CHRONICLES
OF THE
FORBIDDEN

Essays OF Shadow AND Light

By John Nizalowski

ISBN 978-1-5154-1722-4
Copyright 2019 by John Nizalowski

Cover and interior design by NRK Designs

Cover photography
Front: "Ladder"by Paul Zagadka
Back: "Light" by Paul Zagadka

Author biography photo by Kyle Harvey

For information, contact www.iriebooks.com
or
The Editors, Irie Books,
542 Franklin Avenue, Santa Fe, New Mexico 87501

IRIE
BOOKS

Dedication

For Gerald Hausman, who led the way.

ACKNOWLEDGMENTS

These essays have previously appeared in the following publications:

"Night in World's Center."
Weber: The Contemporary West. 32.1. Fall, 2015.

"Four Meditations on the Death of John Lennon."
HARP. December, 1993.

"The Ephemeral Hours."
Digital Americana. Fall, 2013.

"Angels of Bone."
Madblood. August, 2006.

"The Carnival Journey."
Under the Sun. Issue #5. August, 2017.

"Nights at the Burnt Horses."
Malpaís Review. Spring, 2016.

"On the Air."
Dark Matter: A Journal of Speculative Writing.
Issue #7. May, 2015.

"Journeywork of the Stars."
Dark Matter: A Journal of Natural Metaphor. Issue #10.
Winter 2016/2017.

"To a Destination Unknown."
Under the Sun. Issue #3. June, 2015.

CONTENTS

PART ONE

A Great Waiting Silence

"There were just two men under a lamp,
and around them a great waiting silence.
Out to the ends of the universe,
I thought fleetingly, that's the way with man and his lamps.
One has to huddle in, there's so little light and so much space."
– Loren Eiseley, *The Star Thrower*

CHRONICLES OF THE FORBIDDEN

"With this . . . Covarrubias opens his definition to the biblical and patristic condemnation of curiosity as the illicit yearning to know what is forbidden."
— Alberto Manguel, *Curiosity*

I

In the autumn of 1912, archeologist Nels Nelson was exploring the hills just south of New Mexico's Pueblo Largo, a ruined stone city built by the Tewa Indians in the 13th century. Above, the sun blazed from within a hazy white sky, its light washing out the landscape's finer details. To the west, the Ortiz Mountains were a series of dark blue tents pitched on the broad desert plain named by the Spanish cartographers the Galisteo Basin. These lowlands encompassed miles upon miles of juniper covered mounds, mesas, and dry arroyos that stretched north from the Ortiz Mountains to finally wash ashore against the high, snow dusted Sangre de Cristo peaks. The Galisteo Creek bisected this arid world, a wavering silver line that ran westward to vanish into the sandy Cerrillos Hills, where, centuries before the Spanish colonization, the Tewa Indians mined turquoise and transported it hundreds of miles south to the great trading city of Paquimé.

Nelson had been excavating the ruins of Pueblo Largo, and knowing the pattern of the Galisteo Basin's ancient villages, he expected to discover shrines in the surrounding hills. Still, when he had climbed up into these piñon and sage shrouded knolls, he was surprised by a major find – an intact shrine with a "C" shaped chest-high wall of sandstone slabs enclosing nearly 30 square feet, dry-fitted and neatly interconnected, its opening to the east – much like illustrations Nelson had seen of the Minoan shrine at Agia Triada. Then, as he entered the sacred space, he took a sudden, surprised breath. Propped against the shrine's southwest wall stood a seven-foot-high stone slab, and on it, a long dead Tewa priest had carved a four foot high image of a lion-deity, with peaked ears, dots for eyes, a tail, jaguar feet, and outspread arms. A mysterious vertical slit pierced its chest.

This was a rare find indeed. In the early centuries of their colonial occupation, the fervently Catholic Spanish had destroyed most of the basin's sacred stone statuary and stele, perceiving them to be blasphemous. So Nelson believed he needed to ship the ancient stone image to the American Museum of Natural History in New York City as soon as possible, before it was damaged or stolen.

Nelson sent one of his laborers back to the main camp near Pueblo Largo to fetch a wagon. He then directed several other workers, all of them farmers of Spanish descent from the nearby village of Galisteo, to dig out the stele and set it on the ground. With practiced taps of his geologist's hammer, Nelson broke off the top and bottom portions of the slab so it could be more easily packed and shipped back east. Upon completing his task, he regretted his actions. Now shorter than a man, the diminished stele seemed bereft of its power.

By the time the wagon arrived with its paired draft horses the color of polished mahogany, the October sun was nearly behind the Ortiz peaks. Accompanied by diaphanous sheets of sand, a sharp west wind had begun to blow, bringing heavier clouds that blazed orange in the dying light. With the dust stinging their eyes, the men carefully lifted the stele, placed it on a canvas tarp, and then folded the tarp over it. Next, beside the prostrate stele, they placed a set of fragments from a smaller slab inscribed with its own version of the lion-deity. Nelson had found these stone pieces scattered around the hilltop shrine. After the workers placed a final piece of dull grey canvas on the load, the groaning wagon descended the roadless hill towards the main camp. The archeologist and his men followed, shovels resting on their shoulders.

That night, Nelson placed the diminutive slabs with their broken image of the lion deity under his pillow. He told himself he was doing this to protect the images, even though there had never been a single theft during the entire expedition. Despite the October night's penetrating chill, an exhausted Nelson dropped almost immediately into a deep slumber.

At three a.m. he woke from dreams of flying so vivid that even years later he swore his body had hit the pallet just as his eyes snapped open. In the moonlight pouring through the open tent flap, he gathered the stones from under his pillow and stacked them outside. Returning to his bed, he stared at the tent ceiling and speculated that the lion image on the stone stele was a sky deity, and that was why, upon placing the disjointed god-image under his pillow, he had experienced such vivid dreams of flying. Eventually his heart calmed, his eyes closed, and he slipped into a dreamless sleep.

Upon waking at dawn, Nelson, anxious to get the stele out of camp and safely on their way to the museum, decided to take them north to the train station that very day. After breakfast, he joined the teamster on the hardwood wagon seat, and they began the ten mile journey to the rail junction at Lamy. It was slow going. For most of the way there were no roads, so they traversed the dry wash of the Cañada Estacada, bumping over rocks and sliding through the sand.

Around noon, they left the wash and began crossing an open stretch of prairie. Just as they passed a basaltic dike, its black stone wedge looming ominously above the puny wagon, it began to rain. That morning, before departing Pueblo Largo ruins, they had seen dark clouds far to the west, but overhead the blue, windless sky had promised good weather all the way to Lamy. Now, the skies were overcast from horizon to horizon, and grey curtains of precipitation enveloped the western mountains. Before long the light rain became a torrent, the nearby arroyos filled with frothing water, and the wagon's iron-bound wheels began to slip in the mud. They desperately needed shelter, but with no habitations in sight, they pressed on.

The deluge worsened. Pummeled by sheets of heavy rain, they grimly followed a set of wagon ruts heading north. When the lightning started, great, blinding flashes rent the sky from horizon to horizon. Jagged bolts struck the nearby mesas, the stone dike behind them, and finally a dead juniper a dozen yards away with a detonation as loud as the end of time. The horses reared, nearly toppling the wagon. The air filled with the sharp tang of ozone. Another strike, and another. As the teamster desperately pulled in on the reins, it came to the archeologist that he was going to die, that the canvas wrapped god in the wagon was enraged at being violated, truncated, and hauled away to an alien land.

Later, when he had survived the tempest and loaded the precious carved stele onto the train at Lamy, Nelson would explain the source of the storm in a letter sent to the American Museum of Natural History, and later reprinted by Lucy R. Lippard in her book, *Down Country: The Tano of the Galisteo Basin*

– "[We] had desecrated the ancient shrine of a great god, whose image we had laid our hands upon and were carrying away with us."

Nels Nelson had encountered the forbidden.

II

Downstream from Pueblo Largo, just off the Galisteo Creek, rests the town of Los Cerrillos. Back in the late 1980's, when I lived in Santa Fe, Los Cerrillos was a classic western village of adobe or wood-framed houses and storefronts, complete with dusty cottonwoods and old dogs sleeping in the dirt streets. To reach Los Cerrillos, you take the main route from Santa Fe to Tijera, and just as the highway begins to ascend the Ortiz Mountains, you cut off on a gravel county road to the right. In those days, that gravel road changed to packed dirt within Los Cerrillos, and then plunged westward into the volcanic Cerrillos Hills.

The Cerrillos Hills are a place of eerie magic, where grass covered mounds and bluffs surround centuries-old adobe ranch houses tucked into folds of the earth decorated by scattered cattle, sheep, jackrabbits, and antelope. In these ancient hills, the Pueblo Indians mined turquoise at a site called Mount Chalchihuitl. The sacred blue stones produced here have been found as far away as Tula, the thousand-year-old Toltec capital in the central Mexican highlands. When the Spanish arrived in the late 16th century, they kept the mines open, using the Pueblo Indians as slaves to extract the turquoise from their own sacred mountain. In 1680, a group of enslaved

Pueblos died in a mine collapse, and their deaths may have helped spark the great Pueblo Rebellion, which drove the Spanish colonists out of northern New Mexico for twelve years. Not far from these turquoise mines, one of the Cerrillos Hills has a gash in the side, a place of steep cliffs and darkly eroded volcanic stone. I found this place especially intriguing, and I used to enjoy hiking up its narrow, stony gulches, or around and up onto its gentler, west-facing slopes.

One sun-warmed October day, I parked my truck and climbed the rounded side of this sharp-faced hill. At the summit, I headed away from the cliffs, crossing a broad, dry expanse that drifted downward towards a shallow, sandy wash off to the west. The area was over-grazed, and only lonely patches of wheatgrass struggled through the hard, grey soil. However, as is often the case in such places, the cholla cactus thrived. Looking like spiny, petrified snakes, some reached higher than my head. When a cholla dies, its spine transforms into a stiff, lightweight staff punctured by a matrix of narrow oval holes.

I had long wanted one of these staffs, and finding myself surrounded by cholla, I began to search for one. Within moments, I discovered an intact spine resting on the ground next to an altar-sized sandstone slab. About as long as my leg, it was a fine specimen, and I was looking forward to setting it in the living room corner next to my big brown armchair. Since cholla staffs are almost dream-like in their lightness, I lifted it off the ground in one smooth, effortless motion.

Just then I heard a voice. Harsh and distorted, it was surprisingly loud, as if someone were growling next to my ear.

Startled, I dropped the dead cactus and peered quickly around me. There was not a soul in sight, only the rolling, high desert landscape of juniper, piñon, saltbush, and cactus stretching out for miles. High overhead, shining clouds of glaring white and pale yellow concealed the sheltering sky beyond. I don't know why I looked to the heavens, for nothing up there could have been the voice's source, unless one of the ravens drifting in the thermals had somehow amplified its rasping call.

Dropping my gaze, I studied the cholla staff on the stricken ground. The voice had been unnerving, but I wanted that cactus. Peering around the land-scape one more time, I found nothing. The voice had obviously been a trick of my imagination, or some odd acoustic effect of the desert. I picked up the spine again. Silence. Gripping the cholla firmly in my right hand, I set off in the direc-tion of my parked pick-up.

I had walked maybe ten steps when I heard the voice once more, snarling and grinding in my ear. Again I dropped the spine, and again the voice ceased.

Now I was beginning to feel fear.

I abandoned the cactus staff and began moving quickly across the land, reaching in moments a dry wash filled with sand and rounded stones. I followed the wash downstream since I knew it would bisect the Los Cerrillos road near where I'd left my truck.

Despite the uncertainty of my footing on the arroyo's pebbly surface, I moved at a steady pace while the blazing light in the sky sidled towards the blue outline of the Jemez Mountains. The further I travelled from the place of the voice, the calmer I became. Once more I embraced the explanation that either imagination or some trick of the wind had created the sinister sound, though the afternoon was perfectly still.

Finally, I reached a place where the arroyo's walls rose above my head, cutting off my view of the land. Needing to see where I was going, I scrambled up the arroyo's crumbling dirt embankment and emerged onto a gentle rise covered in cholla and shadscale. I was relieved to see my pick-up, a small white Toyota, resting several hundred yards away just off the dirt road to Cerrillos.

I set out for the truck, and about halfway there, I noticed a scattering of small but interesting stones. Some were hard, reddish pebbles, like garnets, and others were formed from a cream-colored rock which had eroded into strange, surreal shapes, like tiny alien skulls. Remembering the voice, I hesitated, but my fascination for unusual desert stones overcame my unease, and I quickly gathered up the most intriguing of these stones and placed them in my pocket. Then I walked the rest of the way to the pick-up.

By the time I reached Santa Fe, dusk had fallen. I pulled off of Paseo de Peralta and onto Castillo Place, the narrow alley where I lived. I parked the pick-up in front of our four room adobe and went inside. The house was wrapped in shadows. In the half-light I crossed the living room, down a short hallway, through the kitchen with its 1950's-era appliances, and into the main bedroom. The window was closed and the shades drawn, so the chamber seemed to hover suspended in a deep, twilit gloom.

My wife of those days, Patricia, was lying in bed, taking a nap. I moved quietly up to the night-table beside the bed, reached into my pocket, and gently placed on it the odd pebbles I had gathered in the Cerrillos Hills. To my surprise, they rattled loudly as they hit the table's wood surface.

"What was that?" Patricia asked sharply, her eyes suddenly wide open, her head and torso rising from the bed. Her round, Slavic face, framed by long brown hair, was troubled. She yanked the chain that lit the lamp resting on the night-table. The pebbles lay clustered under the shaded light, like runes cast for a divination.

"These are stones I picked up near the Cerrillos Hills," I explained.

Propping herself on one elbow, she studied the pebbles, frowning. The red ones reflected the light, but the ones like tiny skulls absorbed it, remaining chalky and dull looking.

"They sounded like bones hitting the table," she said, her voice tense.

"Sorry. I didn't mean to wake you."

As she studied the stones, Patricia's brown eyes grew darker.

"Please get those out of here," she ordered. "They make me very uneasy."

"All right. I'll put them on the kitchen table."

"No!" she nearly shouted. "I want them out of the house."

Nodding, I scooped up the clattering stones and slipped them back in my pocket. Snapping off the light, I made my way back through the house and out onto the front porch. Across the way, a set of small adobe homes lined the alley. The newly lit streetlights were humming in the quiet Sunday evening. I wondered where I could take the cursed stones. It was too dark to drive back to the Cerrillos Hills and return them to their place of origin. I decided to bury them in the backyard. As I left the porch to circle around the house, I glanced up the rise past my landlord's place towards Fort Marcy Hill. The sight of the hill made me stop. I could just make out at its summit the great Cross of the Martyrs, raised in commemoration of the 21 Franciscan priests and friars killed during the Pueblo Revolt of 1680. After a moment's meditation, I decided to bury the darkly mysterious stones near the crucifix.

Walking the short length of Castillo Place to Paseo de Peralta, I followed its westward curve. Most of the brick and adobe houses were dark, though here and there a curtained window cast a gauzy light into the night. I soon reached the asphalt path leading up Fort Marcy Hill and climbed to the cross. Ten-foot-high, the white painted steel cross loomed in the dim streetlight ascending from below. With the cross to my back, I found a bare patch of earth in the park's high desert plantings. There, I dug a small hole with the help of a flat rock, and dropped the stones into it, their infernal clatter dulled by the soft earth. As I covered them, I remembered the growling, other-worldly voice from the Cerrillos Hills.

After finishing the burial, I stood and looked out across Santa Fe spread out before me in the early evening darkness, its avenues and alleys lined with streetlamps, its homes and buildings punctured by squares of golden light. The scattered traffic sounded like a gentle surf, a calming sound. But I couldn't get the sinister voice out of my head, nor the sound of the stones rattling on the bedside table. I felt cursed, like I had violated a place wounded and powerful.

Turning, I studied the cross, the monument to the 21 slain Catholic priests, and their deaths reminded me of the Pueblo Indian slaves who had perished horribly in the turquoise mines of Mount Chalchihuitl. It came to me that I had heard the voices of those Pueblo miners in the Cerrillos Hills, that the agony of being buried alive had left a psychic scar so deep that it had resonated across the centuries to become manifest in the sunlit desert air, the desiccated cactus skeletons, the wind-carved stones of the dry streambed. In that moment, as I peered across the darkened city, this explanation felt very real, and I shivered in the cool autumnal night.

From that moment, I felt a deep shadow envelop my spirit that did not dissipate until I left New Mexico ten months later. And in all the years that have passed since this mysterious encounter, I can still vividly recall those ancient, disquieting voices, and I have never again entered the Cerrillos Hills.

III

Sixty miles northwest of Cerrillos, in the cottonwood bosque of the Rio Grande Valley, there stands the 13th century pueblo of San Ildefonso. This stone and adobe-walled village is divided into two sections, each representing the separate winter and summer sacred societies that shape the socio-religious rituals of the Tanoan people. Just west of the pueblo, the Rio Grande flows over smooth, silt-covered stones past dense groves of cottonwood and Russian olive trees. To the north rises the dark volcanic mound of Black Mesa, a place of holy power forbidden to outsiders. At the pueblo's center, the arms of the village's two sections form a plaza where sacred dances are held. In this plaza, the walls of a great kiva rise into the high desert sun. Most of the kiva's cylinder rests beneath the earth, but about ten feet of it emerges from the ground. A stone stairway ascends to the roof, where a ladder descends into the kiva's depths through a rectangular opening. Within, priests perform secret rites in front of a centuries old carved and painted wood altar, and the people of San Ildefonso prepare themselves for their ceremonies to the sun and the earth, the rain and the stars.

One afternoon, about a year before my encounter with the disturbing voices of the Cerrillos Hills, I was driving along New Mexico Route 502, returning to Santa Fe from a long hike in the Valles Caldera of the Jemez Mountains. The sun was low over the soft mountains behind me, bathing the pair of bridges that span the Rio Grande at Otowi Crossing in a golden light. I crossed the new bridge and came to the turn-off to San Ildefonso. Influenced by the beautiful light and the tired but satisfied glow I feel from long wilderness hikes, I abruptly decided to start down the narrow paved road towards the pueblo. Soon after the road changed to dirt, I reached a rutted parking area just outside the pueblo walls.

Guided by my previous visits to attend the sacred dances at San Ildefonso, I found my way to the plaza. There, in the dying sunlight, stood the kiva. A sudden desire to touch its walls compelled me forward through the pueblo's now vacant square. I knew the kiva was forbidden to me, so I conspicuously avoided the inset stone steps leading to its roof entrance and circled instead to the west wall. For a moment, I placed my open palms on the rough stucco walls, warm in the last rays of the sun. Then, with my back to the curved wall, I sat down and closed my eyes, breathing in the numinous silence. Gradually, I felt a subtle vibration at my back, as if I were sitting against the walls of an electric dynamo, and a deep sense of repose, very much like meditating in a Buddhist temple, flowed into my senses.

A sound like a branch being dragged across the nearby sandy ground broke through my calm. I opened my eyes. The plaza was no longer empty. Across the way, a stooped woman in a long black skirt and tan blouse was passing into an alley, a rust-orange bundle under one arm, a black short-haired dog following close at her heels. Nearby, a tall thin man with a long grey braid, faded blue headband, and bright red flannel shirt was crossing the plaza from west to east. His pace was deliberate, his wrinkled face set in a frown. Beyond him, a young man in blue jeans and a new denim shirt, his hair loose like a dark waterfall, peered off to the north, as if studying Black Mesa's summit. I could not make out what had made the strange sound.

I reclosed my eyes. Time passed. The sun's glow on my eyelids vanished, leaving me in darkness. The vibrations finally returned, but the peace from before eluded me. Instead, I felt increasingly nervous, as if someone were gazing right into my face from just a few feet away. My eyes snapped open. The plaza was again empty. No one was in sight. And yet the feeling of being watched grew stronger.

I was reminded of a rather disturbing discovery I had made on a hike several weeks earlier. I had been exploring a ruined mesa-top pueblo about a dozen miles west of San Ildefonso, a place most likely inhabited by their ancestors. The ruin's stone walls, only a few feet high, outlined room blocks along the mesa's edge and down into the south facing cliffs, where hollowed out spaces held carved niches and smoke-stained ceilings. I had been to this ruin several times before, but I had never followed the cliff past where the ancient pueblo ended. However, there was still plenty of daylight left, so I decided to push past the pueblo boundary to see if there was anything of interest around the curve of the mesa's ramparts.

The mesa and the ruins were formed from a soft, cream-colored stone created from the compressed debris of the Valles Caldera volcano, and across the mesa's south face, there was a ledge along which the Tanoans had built their cliff dwellings. I followed this ledge away from the man-made stone chambers and towards a grove of ponderosa pines. At first the mesa walls beyond the ruins were just blank white walls of volcanic stone.

Then, as the ledge narrowed to about the size of a broad sidewalk, I began to find petroglyphs. At first they were classic Puebloan images – stair-step cloud terraces, tasseled cornstalks, a horned serpent, a few shields with star-shapes within concentric circles. But just as the ledge dwindled to an almost uncomfortable width, I encountered a series of enormous mask-like faces deeply carved into the soft stone. Nearly as high as the cliff walls, these masks were grimacing, sharp-toothed gods clearly angry at what they saw. The final mask was the most fierce of all, its goggle eyes drilling death into the pure blue air. I'd rarely seen such menacing petroglyphs, and never near a pueblo, ruined or inhabited. This made me wonder, why would the Tanoans carve such terrifying visages so close to their dwellings?

I pushed along the diminishing path, and the masks passed from my view around a bulge in the mesa's cliff-face. Then, just before the ledge gave out, I found my answer. Facing southeast, there was a hastily carved larger-than-life Spanish soldier – complete with bandolier, peaked helmet, and sword – astride a horse that could have been torn from Picasso's *Guernica*.

Seeing that soldier made me realize that the masks were for protection, that their terrifying visages sent curses towards Santa Fe, the colonial capital of Northern New Spain, from where bands of soldiers would ride forth to collect tribute and round up conscripted workers for the priests and hidalgos of the territorial settlements, like those Pueblo Indians who had died in the turquoise mines of Mount Chalchihuitl in the Cerrillos Hills.

And just as that 17th century Spanish soldier was an intruder in the divine world of that ancient pueblo, so was I an intruder in the sacred space of San Ildefonso. Unwelcome and unbidden, I knew I should leave. Standing, I placed my hands once more on the rough walls to feel the kiva's holy energy one last time. Then, without glancing back, I left the plaza and the pueblo, got in my pick-up, and headed east down the now darkened highway towards Santa Fe.

IV

Higher up the Parajito Plateau, above the mesa where those ancient Tanoans carved their militant masks to curse the Spanish, there stands in a once verdant forest meadow the city of Los Alamos. Here, in facilities locked away from the outside world, the scientists and technicians of the Manhattan Project, led by physicist Robert Oppenheimer, created the first atomic bomb. On July 16, 1945, at a place named Trinity Site, they detonated this nuclear device, which burned at its moment of ignition hotter than the sun.

Located about 200 miles south of Los Alamos, Trinity Site stands at the head of a long, dry valley that the Spanish called Jornada del Muerto. How the valley acquired this name has much to do with forbidden knowledge. According to historian Paul Horgan, in the early 1600's, a Court of the Inquisition imprisoned a German trader in Santa Fe on the charge of sorcery. This sorcerer escaped with the help of a Pueblo Indian accomplice, and the pair fled south towards El Paso. Although the Indian avoided capture, Spanish soldiers did catch up with the German witch. They found him dead, a pile of animal gnawed bones in that desert valley between the Rio Grande and the Sierra Oscura. And thus, those soldiers named the valley Jornada del Muerto, the Dead Man's March, or the Journey of Death.

I have long been captivated by the history of the Manhattan Project and the first atomic detonations, in part because that history has a personal dimension. My father was in the Navy in the Second World War, and he was assigned to pilot a landing craft for the first wave in the invasion of Japan. The Pentagon expected that initial wave of soldiers and sailors would suffer a ninety percent casualty rate. Therefore, my father believed the atomic bomb saved his life, and while I understood his conviction, I have long been troubled by the atomic devastation of Hiroshima and Nagasaki, and by the bomb's post-war development. Thus, for me, Trinity evokes many contrary aspects of the atomic bomb – the brilliant efforts of the world's greatest physicists to produce a nuclear device in response to German and Japanese authoritarian aggression, the horror of its use on Hiroshima and Nagasaki, Cold War tensions, and the frenzied, fear-driven atomic testing of the 50's and 60's.

But finally, I am both deeply unnerved and fascinated by the strange and terrible power of nuclear weaponry. Atomic detonations tear at the fabric of reality, unleashing stellar energies on the earth's surface so dazzling they can be seen from another world. Indeed, many of the physicists and military personal who witnessed the Trinity test used mythological imagery to describe the experience, as if they had awakened deities of universal destruction. For instance, Robert Oppenheimer evoked the Hindu gods at war to describe the pyrotechnic violence of the first nuclear detonation. "We knew the world would not be the same," Oppenheimer said in a television interview from the early 1960's. "A few people laughed, a few people cried. Most people were silent. I remembered the line from the Hindu scripture, the *Bhagavad-Gita*: Vishnu is trying to persuade the prince that he should do his duty and to impress him he takes on his multi-armed form and says, 'Now I am become Death, the destroyer of worlds.'"

≈≈≈

Many years ago, I made a pilgrimage to Trinity Site.

It was an unusually cold October day as I drove east on U.S. 380 towards Bingham, New Mexico. Ahead, heavy snow-filled clouds devoured the rugged Oscura Mountains, and the sagebrush prairie around me looked bitter and damp. Above, high elevation clouds were thinning, letting in light from a wan, polarized sun. Despite the weather, a long line of cars streamed through Stallion's Gate. Back in 1945, it had been the main entryway used byManhattan Project personnel to reach Trinity. Now it is the north entrance to the White Sands Missile Range.

Joining the caravan, I headed south to a glass and aluminum guard booth where an Air Force airman sporting a dark brown crew-cut handed me a printed flier warning against rattlesnakes and heat exhaustion. It also strictly forbade protesting at Trinity Site or stopping anywhere along the route to Ground Zero. If your car broke down, you were to stay in the vehicle and wait for the MP's to rescue you. The direst warnings concerned taking photos anywhere but at the historic atomic bomb sites, for secret weapon projects were in progress at White Sands, and to record them was absolutely taboo, a heavily punished violation of national security.

After receiving my litany of warnings, I left the booth and drove down an arrow-straight paved road through prairie grass, sage, and yucca. Off in the distance, clustered on or near some low volcanic hills, I spotted a set of white domes, a five-story array of mirrors, a scattering of trailers named the Permanent High Explosives Test Site, and other prohibited mysteries of the White Sands Missile Range. A powerful temptation to stop and study these places seized me, but knowing I would be escorted off the range or even arrested, I repressed the urge and settled for glimpses of these inscrutable structures in my rearview mirrors.

After a seventeen-mile drive, I arrived at a dirt parking lot. Climbing out of my pick-up, I found the air was indeed damp and cold, with a chill breeze blowing from the northwest. The storm clouds over the long line of the Oscura Mountains were getting heavier, yet the cloud cover overhead was thinning, the sunlight growing stronger. I followed the other visitors towards Ground Zero, where the first atomic bomb was detonated. The visitors were an interesting blend, including a heavyset woman with a sweatshirt emblazoned with the Rolling Stones tongue, a strikingly handsome man with a long, blond ponytail, a dapper fellow who spoke with a Russian accent, and several retirees in slacks, windbreakers, and baseball caps

We passed down a dirt road that led to a cluster of vendors selling everything from books about the atomic bomb to mugs decorated with a cloud emblazoned with a blue star and a lightning bolt shattering a yellow sphere into three jagged pieces – the U.S. Army's symbol for the Manhattan Project. Next to the vendors loomed "Jumbo," an enormous cylindrical steel container built to surround the first atomic bomb and catch its precious plutonium if the test had failed. Ultimately, Oppenheimer rejected this plan, and its battered condition is the result of a conventional explosives test performed years later.

Passing Jumbo, I began the long walk down the corridor of fences that leads to Ground Zero. Except for having more grass, the fenced in area looked identical to the prairie beyond. But as Ground Zero approached, I noticed a strange effect – the valley floor was slowly disappearing behind the blast crater's rim, a subtle but unnerving experience.

Just past the entrance to Ground Zero, a gaggle of elderly volunteers, mostly male, stood behind a table with everyday objects that emit radioactivity – glow-in-the-dark clocks, smoke alarms, and the like. The point of this display was to show that these objects were more radioactive than Trinity site, and indeed, when one of these volunteers pointed a Geiger counter wand at one of these household items, the device's rate of clicking would noticeably increase from the lazy rhythms produced by the site's low-level background radiation.

Walking past the table, I reached the crater's center and stood before its volcanic stone obelisk. On this obelisk there is a bronze plaque which states, "Trinity Site – Where the World's First Nuclear Device Was Exploded on July 16, 1945." Nearby, the earth holds the melted remains of a footing from the 100-foot bomb tower. Next, a mock-up of the Fatman plutonium bomb, the kind tested at Trinity and later used on Nagasaki, sits on a flatbed trailer. Beyond Fatman, a series of photos from the Trinity test were arranged along the fence.

The photos began near a low wood and metal shelter that preserves under dusty glass the original condition of ground at Trinity Site after the nuclear detonation. I gazed down at dark colored soil stripped of vegetation. Scattered throughout the dead earth were little green stones, pitted and cratered like a planetarium's model for a small moon. Formed when the nuclear blast fused the desert sand into glass, these stones were pieces of Trinitite, the only objects at Trinity considered dangerous. First, they are radioactive and can cause harm after a long period of direct exposure to the body. However, more troubling than the radiation, Trinitite frequently contains motes of plutonium, and a mere speck of this toxic substance can cause a great deal of damage or even death upon entering one's lungs or bloodstream. Therefore, it is forbidden to take Trinitite from Ground Zero, or to even hold these little green glass stones created in the world's first nuclear fire.

After gazing at the Trinitite for some time, I turned away from the display and watched the tourists milling about with their cameras. Most of them looked bored, and I guessed they had expected something more dramatic. I also noted the positions of the various military personnel, especially the MP's who were making sure none of the guests wandered off into the prohibited zones. Most of them were clustered around the obelisk and the corridor through the fence, since that's where the bulk of the visitors were congregated.

Finally, guided by my research on Trinity Site, I set off towards the perimeter fence as far from the obelisk as I could manage. Out there, away from trails and sightseers, the grass grew more thickly. Without bending over or squatting, which would have attracted the attention of the MP's, I searched the sandy ground amidst the dry stalks. After maybe ten minutes my quest was fulfilled. Between two clumps of bunch grass there rested a dusty grey-green piece of glass. Trinitite.

Despite the posted warnings, I snatched the glass lump and held it in my palm. Slightly warm against my skin, it glinted dully in the cloud-filtered sunlight, its smooth surface pitted and cratered. I pictured that July morning when an impossible blaze fused the sand into a sheet of green glass, a part of which I now balanced on my hand, and I nearly dropped the Trinitite into my shirt pocket. But then I remembered images of Hiroshima taken after the nuclear devastation – skulls seared white in atomic fire, twisted girders bent by a giant's hand, blast burns on an elementary school wall, mounds of brick rubble heaped upon blackened, seared bodies.

Grimacing, I dropped the glass shard back amongst the sere grasses. I stood for a time gazing out at the obelisk, the crowds, and the clouds massed above the distant mountains. Then, with a final glance at the Trinitite shard at my feet, I walked away.

V

The atomic bomb that forged the Trinitite from the Jornada del Muerto desert sands did so by slamming two hemispheres of plutonium together, resulting in a searing atomic fire. Plutonium, the first man-made element, is extracted from uranium in massive chemical separation systems and nuclear reactors. The uranium used to produce the Trinity bomb's plutonium originated in Uravan, a small mining town in western Colorado.

Nestled within the sandstone cliffs of Hieroglyphic Canyon, which cuts through the western edge of the Uncompahgre Plateau, Uravan's mines originally opened in 1899 to produce carnotite, a mineral rich in vanadium, uranium, and most importantly, radium, which had been recently discovered by Marie Curie. For the next twenty years, most of the radium Curie used in her research came from Hieroglyphic Canyon. In those days, the mine operators discarded the vanadium and uranium with the slag.

In 1921, competition from richer radium sources in the Belgian Congo shut down the carnotite mines on the Uncompahgre Plateau. However, by the mid-1930's vanadium became increasingly important in steel production, and a company called U.S. Vanadium re-opened the carnotite mines and built a town named Uravan for the elements uranium and vanadium. In 1944, at the request of the Manhattan Project, Uravan began mining and milling uranium for the atomic enterprise. This activity would continue until 1984, when Uravan's uranium mines and mill were shut down for good. In 1986, the EPA declared that Uravan was the most irradiated town in America, and except for a few buildings preserved for historical posterity, work crews pulverized the entire village – homes, schools, post office, and businesses – and buried the remains under mounds of rock and clay.

A hundred miles north of Uravan, the Uncompahgre Plateau pours into the Grand Valley in a massive, downward arc flowing in slow time. This northern reach of the Uncompahgre Plateau shares much of Uravan's geology and history, including actively producing the raw elements for atomic weaponry. The nation's most important uranium mill, the Climax, was constructed on a former sugar beet mill in the city of Grand Junction, alongside the Colorado River. The mill operated from 1950 to 1970, and during those two decades it produced over two million tons of uranium tailings. At the time, the level of radioactivity in these tailings was deemed safe, so the mill donated 300,000 tons of processed tailings to the city for use in construction. These tailings ended up in the foundational structures of streets, roads, sewers, bridges, embankments, buildings, and houses.

Then, not long after the Climax Mill shut down, the Public Health Service determined that the level of radiation in its tailings was actually dangerous to human habitation, and the Department of Energy's Uranium Mill Tailings Remedial Action project, or UMTRA, was set in motion. By 2000, most of these tailings had been removed from the various foundational structures and shipped to a remote desert storage site south of the city. This site is prohibited, its 94 acres guarded by fences adorned by bright yellow signs emblazoned with the triangular symbol warning against radiation. In the mid-90's, when I would drive the 40 miles from Delta to Grand Junction on my way to work, I would see the lines of trucks carrying their radioactive loads to the forbidden UMTRA site. To keep them safe from the busy highway traffic, the UMTRA trucks had their own highway parallel to US 50, their canvas-covered beds mounded with material that could set a Geiger counter crackling.

Even though Grand Junction was the site of the Climax Mill, there were only a handful of uranium mines in the Grand Valley itself. One set of these mines, consisting of several mostly unproductive shafts, is in a place called Devil's Canyon, about fifteen miles northwest of the city. Despite the rumors of scattered radioactive tailings and the canyon's decidedly sinister name, it is one of my favorite places to hike. Usually when I venture into Devil's Canyon, I move along the bottom of the wash, passing through meandering sandstone walls and over a rock floor worn smooth and carved into chutes and pools by centuries of snow-melt and flash floods.

As one travels south, the sandstone layers ascend onto the Uncompahgre Plateau's heights, and the dark Precambrian granite emerges. Here the canyon broadens out, revealing high, sloping sides and a massive cliff-edged bluff that rises into the sky like the prow of a Titan's ship. If you stay in the canyon and go deep into the looming cliffs, their jagged granite sides all grey and black and multifaceted, the way becomes increasingly difficult, necessitating lots of scrambling over truck-sized boulders and sharp ledges. Ultimately, the sky narrows to a blue trickle overhead, and the high wall of a box canyon prevents further progress. And then there's only one direction to head – back north to the canyon's mouth.

However, above and beyond the box canyon's Precambrian granite wall, another canyon begins that cuts many miles further into the plateau's sandstone strata. And right where the box canyon starts, there is a trail that snakes up the cliff to a wide ledge that can transport the explorer into this elevated realm. Occasionally, when I am feeling especially adventurous, I take this trail. Once, when I did so, I entered the natural world's forbidden heart.

I had climbed up from the canyon floor and was passing along the upper canyon's ledge. Here, the trail hugged the sandstone walls and spires. It was about noon on a mid-April day. The sun, made silver by a veil of cirrus clouds, brightly illuminated the saltbush, juniper, and blue-green sage. Along the steep cliffs, the salmon-colored swirls left in the Wingate sandstone by Jurassic winds looked like the brush strokes of a master impressionist. Swallows darted out from stone over-hangs, seeking insects. Every twenty paces or so, newly emerged whiptail lizards would warily survey my progress. A cool breeze flowed down canyon, carrying with it the scent of melting snows from the plateau's heights. Just above the can-yon rim, a waning crescent moon hung like a broken shell bleached by centuries of seawater.

As I hiked along, I kept remembering a disturbing encounter in Black Dragon Wash, a narrow canyon that cuts through Utah's San Rafael Reef – a long ridge of uplifted sandstone that looks like a petrified tidal wave. Where the reef is at its highest, the Black Dragon Wash has carved towering white sandstone cliffs that form mirroring crescent shapes, and it is here that an ancient people archeologists call the Archaic Indians painted rust-red pictographs of shaman and spirit creatures fifty centuries old. Nearly a year back, I had decided to brave the July heat and trek through Black Dragon Wash, mainly because I would have the canyon to myself. I went late in the day so that the lengthening shadows would protect me from Utah's incendiary sun. The hike turned out to be a chal-lenge. In order to endure the 100-degree heat, I made quick dashes through the sun-exposed passages, lingered in the shaded stretches, and drank plenty of water. However, at first I considered the adventure a great success since there was indeed no one else in the canyon.

By seven p.m. I turned back, and the lower canyon, which was completely in shadow, was actually beginning to cool down. So, I sat across from the Archaic pictographs, studying the tall mummy shapes of the shaman and the long-bodied, stretched-necked image of the creature the first Mormon settlers had named the Black Dragon. Without warning, as I was meditating on these mysterious images of an elder faith, a small black bat started diving at my head. I waved it off, thinking it was hunting insects, but it ignored my warning gestures and kept diving. After a few minutes of this unsettling bombardment, I strode down canyon towards the trailhead. For a time the bat kept harassing me, but as soon as the pictographs went out of sight around the canyon's curve, the bat let up and returned to the rock art panel.

I had never experienced such a belligerent bat as this one. As I put distance between me and the pictographs, I speculated that the bat was protecting a nest or its territory, but even with this explanation, I found the bat's behavior surprisingly aggressive. Regardless, I still wanted to enjoy the canyon's deepening shadows, and deciding I was well away from the bat's range, I sat on a boulder with a good view along the canyon floor. Just as I started to feel a new, delightfully cool breeze descending through the gorge, I glanced up canyon and there was the bat, pumping its wings, erratically flying towards me about fifteen feet above the wash. I couldn't believe it. As soon as it came near, it resumed diving at my head, clearing my scalp by inches.

This time I left more quickly. Once more I went down canyon a good stretch and settled on a rock. Now I must certainly be beyond the bat's range, I thought, but sure as death, the bat doggedly appeared around the canyon's bend, flew towards me, and again went on the offensive. A few minutes of this and I made a dash for my car, getting the hell out of Black Dragon Wash as quickly as possible.

Now, as I was hiking in the upper reaches of Devil's Canyon, I recalled that the bat had made me feel that I was an intruder on the sacred solitude of San Rafael Reef. Perhaps the spirits of the Archaic artists had not appreciated my trick of going there in the summer heat when they normally had the canyon to themselves. It did seem significant that the bat had first attacked me at the pictograph site. I also pondered why this memory had arisen so strongly here in Devil's Canyon, a quite different landscape over a hundred miles from Black Dragon Wash. Inexplicably, the scene with the bat kept playing over and over in my mind, as if evoked by the rhythm of my boots on trail's dust and raw stone. Later, I understood – the memory of the bat was a warning of what was to come.

My destination was maybe another two or three miles ahead – an old one-room miner's cabin maintained by the B.L.M. for campers and hunters. Now that I had completed the ascent to the mouth of the upper canyon, I was moving along the mostly level trail at a good clip, and I figured I would reach the cabin in less than an hour.

The trail began to arc around a massive pagoda-shaped sandstone tower. With the pagoda's smooth rock wall beside me, I could not see very far ahead – just the trail's curve and the plunge beside me down ragged cliffs to the dry stream below. But the trail was on level ground, and I could keep up my pace. So when ledge widened and I burst out into a meadow of tall, dusty grasses, I took several long strides before coming to a complete stop.

For there, not ten yards before me, stood a flock of bighorn sheep.

A male built like a block of granite guarded their front. Behind him ranged four or five ewes and a half dozen lambs. Several juvenile males held the flanks and rear. The alpha ram had great, thick horns that formed a full spiral out beyond his head and then curled back to frame his eyes. He was perched on a flat, sandstone slab, and so his head was even with mine. The ewes had narrow, partially-curved horns, and the juvenile males possessed horns that were pale echoes of the alpha male's. They all had velvety-beige hides, white snouts and rumps, and small elfin ears. And in the tense silence, they had all stopped grazing to stare straight at me.

My gaze flicked between the different members of this tribe, until I ultimately focused on the lead ram. His yellow, ancient Egyptian eyes were filled with a wild, untamed power, like the eyes of a madman or a warrior in the heat of battle. They were utterly unlike the eyes of a tame animal, even a pit bull or German shepherd fiercely defending its territory. These eyes held no recognition of the human dimension, no notion of the hominid race as a species to be honored or feared or reckoned with in any way. Glancing again at the ram's severely curved horns, I remembered a time years back, when a bighorn ram had totaled a stopped car on the road near my home in the San Juan Mountains. When I looked back at the ram's eyes, they made the following demand.

You are forbidden from our presence, and you shall not pass. It is taboo for you to be here in the wilderness reaches of Devil's Canyon. Return to your strange world of rectangular houses, unreal lights, and tar highways. We will never be harnessed by human hands. Depart. Depart now.

And so I did. I slowly backed down the trail, easing one foot behind the other, never taking my gaze from the ram. I understood now why the *yei*, the demi-gods of the Navajo, would sometimes appear to shaman in the form of bighorn sheep, for in that moment, this ram was indeed a deity. Finally, when the stone pagoda hid me from the flock, I turned and picked up the pace, urging my now shaky legs to quickly take me from this potent wilderness to my steel and glass automobile so I could return to the comfortable world of streets, locked doors, and fenced-in yards that hides us from the powers of the earth.

VI

In Greco-Roman mythology, perhaps the most powerful warning against violating a taboo of both the sacred and natural worlds is the legend of Actaeon's descent into the cave of Artemis. The story was already thousands of years old when the Greeks wove it into their Bronze Age mythos. We receive it from the first century C.E. poet Ovid, who relates the story of Actaeon in his masterwork, *The Metamorphoses.*

While being a lunar deity, Artemis – the Roman Diana – is in her truest essence the goddess of the wilderness. Her origins reach back to the Paleolithic, when ancient Europeans would depict a goddess of wild animals on their cave walls. She was the creator of dangerous and beautiful forms – antelope, deer, bison, and wild bulls – and the mistress of hunts that could be as deadly for the hunters as for the prey. This Ice Age goddess evolved over thousands of years into Artemis, who the Greeks associated with the bear, the oldest object of human worship.

In the late Neolithic, the farmers who lived in uneasy proximity to the forest, which they both feared and admired, connected Artemis with Selene, the youthful Titan moon goddess, and Hecate, the goddess of witchcraft, to form a version of the Triple Goddess – lover, mother, and crone – the Great Mother who eternally shaped the cycles earth and sky, water and fire. The Bronze Age Aegean Greeks, who viewed the wilderness as a troubling place to either subdue or avoid in their quest to build a patriarchal civilization based on cities and the sword, stripped Artemis of her procreative powers and transformed this once fecund deity into a virgin. Still, Artemis retained her sacred authority over game animals and childbirth, and the Aegeans upheld her power by having her represent the realm of the inviolate feminine, a woman absolutely taboo to men.

And thus the story of Actaeon begins.

≈≈≈

Actaeon, son of Autonoë and Aristaeus, was the grandson of Cadmus, founder of Thebes, the city where Pentheus and Oedipus would play out their tragic lives. A renowned hunter, Actaeon possessed a pack of remarkable hounds that were both implacable when running down prey and utterly loyal to their master. His favorite game animal was the bear, the slaying of which challenged his skills to the utmost and whose flesh provided much meat for the people of Thebes. Indeed, he had erected an altar from the white skulls of his many bear kills.

One warm summer's day, Actaeon penetrated deep into the forest a good day's march south of Thebes, seeking bear. In a woodland meadow, he came across a previously unknown cave in a limestone cliff where Mount Cithaeron begins to rise into the heavens. Its ovoid opening, shaped like a wildcat's eye, held the promise of quarry. So, after lighting one of the torches he carried in a leather sling next to his quiver of iron-tipped arrows, Actaeon pulled his short-sword from its sheath, ordered his hounds to await his return, and entered the cave.

At first, he could see fairly well from the sunlight filtering in through the opening. After the entrance, the cave widened into a great chamber, and then about fifty paces in it narrowed considerably and bent out of sight. The floor was solid stone, which was unfortunate, since there was no soil or debris to leave tracks and confirm the presence of bear. Nor did Actaeon find scat or other bear signs. It did not seem likely he would find his prey here, yet something about the shape of the cave and the mysterious bend up ahead drew the hunter within.

As Actaeon passed through the bend, the light from the outer world ceased. The passage, while becoming wider and narrower in turns, remained just high enough for Actaeon to pass without lowering his torch. He moved cautiously, studying the jagged, dirty-grey stone walls and floor for any animal signs, but found none. Now and then, the stone icicles of stalactites and the strange beehives of stalagmites made his progress difficult. Also, the cave twisted through labyrinthine folds and reversals, and all he had for light was the flickering torch. The damp, cool air smelled of decaying rock and ancient, buried seas. At one point, he traversed a great spherical chamber, the outer reaches of which were beyond his torchlight. Here, a flight of bats startled him, their black-winged forms swooping at him out of the upper darkness.

Penetrating deeper and deeper into the cave, Actaeon kept thinking he should return to the world of daylight and forests, deer and hunting hounds. And yet, he ignored these feelings and went onward. Like Odysseus's desire to hear the song of the Sirens, Actaeon felt a burning curiosity about this serpentine under-world, and he swore to attain the cave's very heart.

At last, he reached a fork. A faint, yellow glow, almost like sunlight, emerged from the left passage, so that was the direction he took. After a series of turns, during which the light grew brighter, he came to a rough, rectangular chamber. At its far end, a series of broad stone steps led to a circular cut in the cave wall. A stream of faintly steaming water ran down one side of the steps to be devoured by a slit in the stone floor. The golden light emerged from this opening, along with the sounds of a gentle waterfall and a fresh, clean scent that reminded Actaeon of his mother Autonoë's mint garden. He also thought he heard wom-en's voices, light and laughing, but he couldn't tell if they were truly voices or the echo of the flowing waters off the cave walls.

Actaeon went forward, stopped at the base of the stone stairs, and listened to the mysterious voices that emanated from above. He felt a deep unease, sens-ing the sacred presence that dwelled beyond the opening at the top of the steps. Once again he almost departed, but his desire to know what lay beyond the illuminated opening was too strong. At long last, he wedged his torch in a fissure in the limestone wall, climbed the stairs, and passed through the almost perfect cylindrical passage.

He found himself in a vast oval chamber, like being inside a great egg. Ranged around the walls, torches burned with an unearthly color – bright fragments of the sun captured on the ends of bronze shafts. The basin of the enormous womb-cave was filled with steaming waters fed from underneath by volcanic springs. And in this underworld lake, illuminated in the shimmering metallic-yellow light, twelve women bathed, their naked bodies taut and athletic, their skin and hair as golden as the flames on the torches.

The moment Actaeon entered, the women fell silent and turned as one to stare at him. Then, from the center of the twelve, a figure emerged. She was taller than the rest, and her body was perfection; it would shame even the finest runners and discus throwers at the Olympic contests. To Actaeon's astonishment, her face possessed an aristocratic beauty that surpassed even Harmonia's, queen of Thebes and descendent of Aphrodite. And that was when his awe and delight gave away to terror, for upon seeing that beatific face and body, Actaeon realized that he was gazing upon Artemis, daughter of Zeus, goddess of the hunt, and that the other twelve women were her sacred band, the virgin huntresses of the forest. Thus, he was a dead man, for the gods had decreed that it was absolutely taboo for a male to witness the naked body of Artemis.

Still, Actaeon could not turn away from the goddess's blue steel eyes, so wild and true and terrifying that they stripped his soul of meaning. Because her golden bow was out of reach in a rack of weapons next to the chamber wall, Artemis dipped her cupped hands in the pool and flung water on the helpless hunter.

"Now flee," she commanded, her voice filling the chamber like the growling of a great she-bear. "And see if you can tell the tale of this, your final hunt."

As the warm waters stuck his face and shoulders, Actaeon's eyesight began to blur, and the cave became both brighter and less distinct. The laugher of the women overpowered his ears as he dropped to all fours. His skin burned and his head split with pain as something grew out of his skull. Suddenly, his vision cleared and he saw again the fearsome, penetrating gaze of the goddess. But now he bolted from those eyes blazing like stars in a chaos devoured sky.

Awkwardly whirling on his new legs, Actaeon ran past his fallen sword and clattered down the stairs back into the rectangular chamber. Near his torch, he passed by a mirror-like stretch of the stream and was shocked to see a stag's head crowned by a set of magnificent antlers reflected in the water. Dashing on, he found he could dimly see his path; the cave was no longer swallowed up in total darkness, as it had been before. Also, he could now smell his way through the labyrinth by tracking a fresh breeze coming from the cave mouth.

Behind him, the calls of the pursuing huntresses drove a wild panic through his very soul, and propelled by this, he rapidly threaded the cavern's maze, barely keeping his footing as he twisted through snaky bends and stalagmite barriers. Just as he began to stagger from fatigue, the cave passage brightened, and the opening appeared. He surged through it, and though the blaze of the summer sun blinded him, he did not pause in his flight for the deep woods.

Then, at the very moment he reached the first sheltering oaks, his own hounds leapt upon him, tearing his flesh. He staggered and dropped, his blood spilling into the decaying leaves of the forest floor. Struggling past searing waves of pain, he tried to order his hounds to cease, but he could only groan in agony with a sound that was neither human nor deer. So wordlessly he died, as his hounds bayed in triumph, calling to their master to witness the kill.

Thus the gods upheld the taboo against violating the secret heart of the natural world – the deep realm of Artemis, undying goddess of nature.

VII

For the Zuni, a Pueblo Indian tribe who dwell in western New Mexico, Ku'yapal-itsa is the goddess of the hunt. Like the slayer of Actaeon, Ku'yapalitsa is a beautiful virgin, mistress of the wilderness, game animals, and childbirth. It is said that she possesses a magic corral near Zuni Salt Lake, and with it she can capture great numbers of antelope and deer. Of these, she slays only the animals she needs for sustenance, and the rest she releases where Zuni hunters may track them so that the people will thrive. However, there is a powerful taboo against finding this corral, and anyone who happens upon it will die within four days.

Thus, the forbidden exists everywhere, across the eons. And whether they are determined by ancient deities, the mysterious forces of the natural world, or the strictures of social order, these taboos are dangerous to challenge. To do so is to risk madness, wounding, or even death – a lightning strike on the Galisteo Basin, a curse from long buried turquoise miners, the wrath of a kiva priest, toxic poisoning by stray molecules of plutonium, the charge of a mountain ram determined to defend his flock. All of these punishments and more are encompassed by Actaeon and his tragic metamorphosis, or the death that arrives from seeing Ku'yapalitsa's enchanted corral.

And yet, despite knowing this, we still cross these boundaries. Some fundamental aspect of the human soul propels us to seize the rain-god stele from the Pueblo Indian altar, sit with our backs to the sacred kiva, handle deadly glass shards from the first atomic fire, penetrate the sacred cave to witness the naked goddess of the untamed universe. We are all Odysseus, tied to the mast, burning with curiosity to hear the song of the Sirens and gain prohibited knowledge.

Occasionally, we acquire this knowledge to save the world – Prometheus robbing Olympus of the fire Zeus forbade humankind, the Navajo Warrior Twins journeying to their Sun Father for the holy weapons needed to slay the monsters ravaging the people, Sir Lancelot seeking the Grail to heal a fractured Camelot, Robert Oppenheimer unleashing atomic violence to prevent fascism from devouring the planet.

But regardless of our motives, there is always a price. Zeus chained Prometheus to a mountain and ordered an eagle to devour the fire-stealer's liver every sunrise. When the Warrior Twins cleared the world of monsters, the spirits of those beasts haunted these Navajo heroes, driving them in misery across the carved plains of the Painted Desert. Lancelot ignored the mysterious voices warning him not to enter the Grail Chapel, and upon seeing the sacred object he was struck blind. During the Communist witch-hunts of the 1950's, the Atomic Energy Commission accused Oppenheimer of being a security risk and stripped him of his clearance, ruining his life and breaking his spirit.

As for me, my encounters with the forbidden have fortunately left me largely unscathed, perhaps because I backed off from the taboo in time. I did not keep the cursed stones of Cerrillos and Trinity; nor did I enter the holy kiva of San Ildefonso, defy the guardian bat of Black Dragon Wash, or provoke the mountain sheep of Devil's Canyon. I am grateful that my mere glimpses into the forbidden have been enough, since they have taught me both the power and peril of Artemis's cave and Ku'yapalitsa's corral.

Most importantly, however, these visions have opened me to the transcendent. They have made me certain that there does exist a deeper, more fundamental reality behind the world's outer aspect. And while I certainly do not fully comprehend this deeper reality, what I have witnessed – the brilliant and sometimes disquieting colors revealed by the scattered tears in the concealing curtain of appearances – has convinced me that the animistic vision held by the earth's tribal peoples is correct. Thus I believe that everything – humans, animals, plants, rivers, valleys, and bluffs; the mountain sheep in a western Colorado canyon, a cholla cactus spine in the Cerrillos Hills, the kiva of a Pueblo Indian village, the very stones that form the kiva, even the green shard of Trinitite in the Jornada del Muerto – possesses spirit.

And as the long arc of mythology and ritual has run its course, the modern world has returned to this incredibly ancient but enduring animist revelation. This is what the Transcendentalists – Whitman, Emerson, and Thoreau – realized, and this is what contemporary science – especially quantum physics and cosmology – proclaims. Set into motion by the Universal Mind, there is no greater miracle than the natural world, from the sublime beauty of the ruby-throated hummingbird pollinating the crimson flowered lobelia, to the searing violence of a supernova. The entire cosmos partakes in the great cycle of destruction and creation – the pollinated flower dies and sheds seeds which germinate and become new flowers, and the supernova spreads the sacred elements across interstellar space that form future stars with planets on which humans evolve and observe the hummingbirds feeding at their backyard blossoms. As Walt Whitman declares in *Song of Myself*, "A leaf of grass is no less than the journeywork of the stars."

This search for the transcendent is why we explore the edges of existence, including those realms the gods have forbidden, and I have done my share of trespassing in those strange lands. However, now that I am approaching my elder years, my rim-skirting adventures are largely behind me, and I tend to stay on the better-lit side of the line between the known world and the realm of the dangerously mysterious. I no longer feel compelled to push the universe's limits, so I am content to wait, for soon enough I will cross that ultimate boundary. At that transitional moment, Hermes will guide my soul to the Styx. Or, since I live in the Americas, perhaps it will be Masau'u, Hopi deity of the underworld, who will take me to that dark river. Once there, I will glide across its smooth, shadowy waters into the kingdom of final knowledge.

Night at World's Center

It was a strange night.

Later, I would learn that I had spent it at the center of the world. But at the time, I only knew I was camping in a place both beautiful and alien, filled with eerie wonder and odd dreams.

Back then, in the mid-1980's, the Blanco trading post stood where the road to the great Pueblo Indian ruins complex at Chaco Canyon cut off from Highway 44, and since it was drizzling, and the guidebooks warned that the Chaco roads could become muddy and impassible in the rain, I decided to stop in for advice.

While Patricia, my wife of those days, waited, I got out of our pickup and headed across a poorly graveled lot towards a low, white cinderblock building with iron grillwork on the windows. Inside, I discovered a surprisingly large room bursting with a amazing variety of goods – racks of Winchester rifles, burlap sacks of beans, coils of rope, stacks of Stetson hats, piles of Pendleton rugs, bridles hanging from the ceiling, and shelves filled with Corn Flakes, jars of sweetened peaches, and Chock Full 'O Nuts coffee in yellow cans. Here and there, slender Navajos in jeans and cowboy shirts looked over the goods. One was hefting a rifle. A boy of about twelve was peering out the window. He seemed to be studying our white Toyota pickup and its Virginia plates. No one looked at me. I was in a very different world from the one I'd grown up in, and it was a world that was beginning to seize my imagination.

Across the back end of the trading post, facing the door, stood a series of glass cases topped by a long oak counter. The cases were crammed with Navajo silver jewelry – bolos, rings, bracelets, and belt buckles. Behind the counter, a tall, stooped, thickset man perched on a stool. His thinning white hair caught the cloudy gray light from the windows and the dim glow of scattered fluorescent tubes overhead. His skin was very pale, with a reddish tinge, like a permanent sunburn. I walked up to the counter, said hello, and asked him if he knew the conditions of the roads to Chaco Canyon.

"No, I sure don't," he said in a voice that was gruff but not unfriendly.

"I heard that they can get slick when it rains. Has it rained enough to be a problem?"

"Couldn't tell ya'. It might have."

"Is there a phone I could use to call the park headquarters?"

"I've only got the radio phone. You're welcome to use it, but it'll cost you ten dollars."

For a moment I thought that he was kidding. His steady gaze and unchanged expression convinced me otherwise.

"No thanks. I guess I'll just try to get there in a day or two."

And that was that. The man said nothing more. I muttered a goodbye and turned to go. The Navajos were silent through the entire exchange. When I got back to Patricia in the truck, I told her what had been said, and we decided to head north on the highway and look for a place to stay the night.

As we drove, the day began to fade, and the cloudy, grey sky grew even darker. Now and then rain spattered the windshield.

"I guess we did the right thing," I said.

"Probably," Patricia answered, her long brown hair and round, pleasantly Slavic face tinged with silver in the polarized light.

"Maybe we should find a motel," I suggested.

For a time, Patricia watched the rain-wet road, an asphalt ribbon stretched out between barren hills and wind-eroded shale bluffs. Most of the cars on the highway had already turned on their lights. The coming nightfall and the rain made the idea of a motel very attractive. But we were on a six-month cross-country sojourn, and motels were costly, a drain on our limited funds.

"What's the next town?" she asked at last.

"Bloomfield."

"Let's see if there's a good place to camp before we reach town. If not, we'll go ahead and get a room."

For us, all of this was new country, and everything was fascinating. We passed a hospital complex with clean white buildings and a tall water tower with black letters that proclaimed in Navajo – *Dzilith-Na-O-Dith-Hle*. Nearby, green fields stretched out towards the west, irrigated by huge wheels connected by aluminum tubes, like a Tinker Toy set of the gods spewing water. But mostly there was a sage vastness broken here and there by ragged piles of shale, their turquoise, blue, and lavender shades vivid in the damp air. I had grown up on New York's lush

Allegheny Plateau, and had just moved from Virginia's Blue Ridge Mountains, where maple, ash, hickory, and oak cover long, rolling ridges, and rhododendrons or thick grasses fill in the few open spaces. By contrast, in New Mexico a scrubby juniper as high as a sagging shed was tree king of an arid empire.

After maybe twenty minutes, we passed a rectangular green sign that read "Bloomfield - 18 Miles," and I figured we would be under motel sheets that night and forty bucks lighter, when another sign flashed by, a brown one with white letters spelling out "Angel Peak." The sign's arrow pointed right. Beneath was another sign bearing a stylized white tent.

I turned to Patricia and with a nod she said, "Let's check it out."

〜〜〜

So we turned back, and a fifteen minute drive down a good dirt road brought us to the Angel Peak campsite. What greeted us, even in the half-light of dusk, was genuinely impressive. It was as if a chasm to the earth's core opened out before us, revealing jagged, wind-carved spires of shale and sandstone, mostly beige in color, that seemed to glow under the silver-gray clouds. At the heart of the abyss stood Angel Peak – a tall spire surmounted by a winged shape that could be anything from an angel to a bat. Scattered across the basin, a few natural gas wells pumped away, the kind that look like Erector Set dinosaurs, stabbing at the earth in a steady up and down rhythm. Somehow, though, they didn't take away from the surreal beauty of what stood before us.

We couldn't believe our luck. The place was intriguing, no one else was there, and at that moment it wasn't raining. Besides, it was a BLM site, so the camping was free. We quickly set up the tent, fired up the Coleman stove, and had a quick supper of instant miso soup and thick pieces of whole grain bread.

By the time we were finished, the light was totally gone. Yet, with the lull in the rain, we decided to sit outside anyway, recounting the day's adventures and watching the far-off flicker of lightning. Insects buzzed and ticked in the dark desert. An occasional animal would scurry in the brush. Finally, we grew tired and crawled into our army surplus sleeping bags. After the usual squirming to find the best dips and folds in the hard ground beneath us, we fell asleep.

≈ ≈ ≈

As I said, it was a strange night, filled by violent storms, odd noises, and broken sleep laced with bizarre dreams.

By midnight, the thunderstorms, which had seemed so far away when we turned in, raged overhead, dumping rain right on us, with wind and lightning all around. When they finally passed, I poked my head out of the tent to find a clear sky scattershot with thousands of stars – Pegasus, Cassiopeia, and the other autumn constellations already past zenith. Soon after, the coyotes, the trickster animals of Navajo mythology, started in. At first, they barked and yapped from a distance. By 3:00 a.m. they were padding across the ground right outside, sniffing at the tent seams, brave in their curiosity.

But far more troubling than the coyotes were the dreams. The ones I remember best were of masked, dark-skinned men walking in a slow procession across a rolling desert far more sandy and barren than the one outside the tent. Their masks were like Maori creations – all loops and spirals the color of dried blood, with big eyes and circular mouths. Upon waking, I would hear the coyotes, and then slide back into the dream – the row of dark figures forever moving across their desert from unseen origin to unknown destination.

I was certainly grateful when the rising sun set the Angel Peak basin aflame. As dawn set the tent wall ablaze with light, we pulled ourselves out of our sleeping bags, lit the Coleman, and started a breakfast of oatmeal and black tea. A few torn, gray clouds scudded across the sky, but largely the heavens had become startling clear and deeply azure, like poured blue ink. As we ate, Patricia and I discussed the coyotes, the thunder, and our dreams. She too had seen strange things in her sleep. Seeking confirmation of the night's occurrences, we searched the ground, but found no tracks. It was as if the coyotes had been phantoms.

It came to me then that something mysterious had happened, that our evening's encounters possessed a numinous quality. That night at Angel Peak – with its unsettling alchemy of the storm's fire, masked dreams, and wild canines – had opened my consciousness to the southwestern desert's magic reality, an interior realm that penetrates appearances and gives them a transcendent depth and texture.

That sacred realm would fully emerge at Chaco Canyon.

≈≈≈

With the warming sun overhead, we didn't stop at the trading post. Instead, we drove down a dirt road towards the once mighty center of the 12th century theocratic civilization of the Anasazi, the deep root of contemporary Pueblo Indian culture. The road bumped and weaved through shale hills past scattered octagonal log hogans and the occasional abandoned car. Here and there, Navajos herded sheep, their scruffy dogs nipping at the heels of strays. Twice we crossed through washes whose wet sandy bottoms made the truck weave as if I were driving through heavy snow. It became clear why the road would be so treacherous in a rainstorm.

An hour of driving brought us to a sign announcing the canyon. There was a sharp turn, a duck-shaped sandstone hoodoo, and then a plunge through a break in the 300-foot canyon walls onto the canyon floor, where the road changed to blacktop. At that time, a traveler entered Chaco from the northwest, past the ruins named Casa Chiquita, Kin Kletso, and Pueblo del Arroyo, their ancient multi-storied stone structures perched on the edge of Chaco Wash's deep sides. Beyond, more ruins dotted the wide sandstone canyon, and we watched them stately pass by as we drove towards the ever looming Fajada Butte, site of the famous sun dagger, a projection of sunlight against a spiral petroglyph that had once marked the solstices and equinoxes before the rocks shifted in 1989.

I had entered the realm of the ancient and powerful, and I felt the changes that had started at Angel Peak grow within me like an exotic flower. An internal compass was shifting, my beloved green hills of Appalachia giving way to the cinnamon deserts of the Southwest.

≈≈≈

We spent three days at Chaco. In that time we explored all of the canyon's major multi-story ruins, called by archeologists the "great houses," several major pueblos beyond the canyon's rim, and a handful of the minor structures.

On our first day, we barely got started. We had decided to explore the canyon systematically, so we began with the ruins closest to the campground. Resting on the rocky slope directly above the glass and stucco visitor's center, Una Vida, a largely unexcavated ruin, was a humble assemblage of crumbling walls and several kivas – the underground circular stone temples within which the Pueblo Indians perform their sacred rites to this day. But since this was our first ruin at Chaco Canyon, we were utterly fascinated, and spent a great deal of time studying the fine workmanship of the walls, with their intricate interconnected stones the size of expensive art books. Our boots whispered on the fine sand covering the stone slabs and trails, while a slight breeze rustled the sage and salt bush. The air had by then lost its rain-washed freshness and possessed instead the flinty smell of heated rock. In the white sky, the sun blazed forth from its zenith, illuminating a set of shining clouds to the east. The few other people visiting Una Vida were, like us, hushed, respectful, sensing that we were in a sacred place, like a medieval cathedral or an Egyptian pharaoh's tomb. From the rise upon which Una Vida stood, there was a sweeping view to the south. There, the canyon opened out into a vast plain dominated by Fajada Butte.

After Una Vida, we drove a mile up-canyon to Hungo Pavi, another medium sized, unexcavated ruin. This one stood almost against the canyon's cliff face, and its structure was more intact, rising in places to nearly three stories. Along its back, facing the cliff, there was a long wall, inset here and there by rectangular windows. This wall gave the structure an impression of size and breadth, and we left feeling great anticipation for the next day's planned exploration of Pueblo Bonito and Chetro Ketl, the largest great houses in the canyon.

That night we stayed in the National Parks Service campground. It spread beneath a high cliff to the west of the canyon's mouth. The campground had its own small, single-story pueblo ruin, and at dusk we sat in it for a time, looking out over the campground's scattering of campfires, humble camper trailers, and nylon tents, their colors – beige, rust-red, dark blue, and dull green – fading in the growing darkness.

As the last light played on Fajada Butte, a man of about fifty joined us in peering out across the early evening's landscape. Wearing jeans and a faded denim shirt, he was short, lean, and wiry, with shoulder-length silver-black hair and goatee. He greeted us in his soft, unassuming voice, and explained that he had spent his life travelling the world, supporting himself as a mechanic, working at jobs just long enough to raise the money to reach his next destination. This was his third visit to Chaco Canyon, one of his favorite places on the planet. He asked us if we had been to Pueblo Bonito yet, and when we told him we planned to go the next day, he nodded and smiled.

"It is a most amazing structure – five stories high and a thousand rooms," he stated in his quiet tones. "And none of it built out of fear, or power, or coercion. Instead, they constructed it from faith, faith in the Sun Father and the spirits of the earth. Just think of it – a thousand years ago these people created the sacred dances and told the holy stories that today's Pueblo Indians still dance and sing."

He paused for a long time, studying the campfires, the vanishing desert scrub, and the stone bluffs. Finally, as he stood to return to his camp, he pronounced his drifter's benediction.

"For all its hardships, it must have been a beautiful life, living here and practicing your ceremonies year after year, knowing your place in the universe. Probably as close to utopia as humankind has ever come."

Later, as I stared into our campfire, watching the flames form phantom shapes that danced and changed, I thought about his words. After the stars came out hard and bright and clear, we entered our tent and I slept a profound, dreamless sleep. It was a sharp contrast to the night at Angel Peak.

≈≈≈

The next morning, we set out to the far northwestern end of the canyon to explore Chetro Ketl and Pueblo Bonito. And these structures, so massive and complex, and yet so pure of line and at one with the land, more than fulfilled the promise made by Una Vida and Hungo Pavi.

When it was completed 1115 C.E., Chetro Ketl consisted of nearly 500 rooms and stood four stories high. Built along the north side of the canyon to take full advantage of the winter sun, Chetro Ketl includes a continuous stone wall that runs for 500 yards. Far greater than the formation that had impressed me at Hungo Pavi, this wall gave me the truest sense of the great size of Chaco Canyon's constructions. As I walked slowly down the wall's length, gazing up at the stonework, peering into its occasional rubble-filled window, the image of that wall, so filled with mysterious power and architectural simplicity, drove deep into my heart.

After Chetro Ketl, we walked the half mile under the blazing late morning sun to the massive five-story, bow-shaped Pueblo Bonito. With 700 rooms and 33 kivas, it is the canyon's apex structure and covers nearly five acres. I remembered the drifter's words about "knowing your place in the universe," while entering its stone depths. There, the multi-layered corridors of connected rooms, rectangular doorways and corner windows evoked for me the Cretan labyrinth at Knossos, or the multi-chambered sacred temple of the Eleusinian Mysteries near Athens. In some of the rooms, cool from the sharp shadows cast by three-story high walls, stone metates lay on the smooth dirt floors, as if awaiting the return of women a thousand years gone to again patiently grind the corn to feed the children playing in the great, arc-shaped courtyard.

But it was during our final day at Chaco Canyon that I encountered the ruin that captivated me most deeply and completed my southwestern metamorphosis.

Casa Rinconada, which stands on a small rise across the wash from Pueblo Bonito, is the largest kiva in Chaco Canyon. Strangely, the pueblo ruins at the base of its slope are rather humble in size and appearance. But the kiva, a grand, circular structure over sixty feet in diameter, is a revelation of the sacred.

When I made this first journey to Chaco, the Parks Service still allowed visitors to enter Casa Rinconada and stand on its sandy floor. Today, Pueblo Indian elders have forbidden such excursions, and for good reason. As I was to discover, Casa Rinconada is a sacred and powerful space and should be respected as such. Today, a prayer stick planted in recent times by a Pueblo Indian priest stands as a sentry against intruders.

But three decades ago, one could descend into the kiva, and so we did, walking slowly down the stairs through the rectangular antechamber in the structure's north side. At the base of the stairs, we ducked under the wall through a small, tight passage, and came out into a spacious circular space. The roof had long been absent, and above there was only the blue sky and the sun of heaven. I stood still for a time, feeling strangely alone and vulnerable down under the earth's surface and surrounded by the great 900-year-old circle of stone. It was as if the infinite horizon had been captured within these rock walls, and the gods would at any moment peer down at me from the kiva's rim to challenge my presence in their temple.

At last, I began to move with measured steps, like when I was an altar boy carrying the crucifix on Holy Friday around the periphery of the church. I walked clockwise around the kiva alongside the wall's low stone ledge and peered into every square chamber built into the wall. Later I found out that there are thirty-four of these niches, and they were created for the storage of sacred objects – copper bells, stone fetishes, eagle feather fans, and other spiritual totems.

Today, all of them are empty. I could hear the sound of my boots crunching on the stone-strewn earth, my steady breathing, and that was all. There was no wind, and Patricia, who stood in the center between the large, earth-filled rectangular vaults constructed from low stone walls, was completely silent.

When I had completed my circumambulation, and I was standing again at the north entrance, I closed my eyes and entered a state similar to Buddhist meditation. I could feel the sun on my face, an aching weariness in my feet and legs, the binding of my watchband.

And then it happened. For a moment, I had a vision of the masked dancers from my dreams at Angel Peak. Then came a rushing sound like an ocean surf, and with it the sensation of flying. Light-headed and dizzy, I couldn't feel my feet on the ground. I believed for all the world that I was hurtling through the sky and into the sun.

Frightened, I snapped open my eyes, and saw Patricia, ten feet away, smiling at me.

"You felt it too."

"Yes," was all I said in answer.

≈ ≈ ≈

As I stood at the great kiva's center, the transcendent vision that had entered my unconscious like a seed during my strange night at Angel Peak sprouted from the Chacoan earth and embraced my soul. Only in the Southwest do I encounter this way of seeing and feeling. For me, this region weaves a reality that is vital and mysterious, beautiful and dangerous. Ever since my stay at Angel Peak, there are certain southwestern places that evoke this deep vision, from the gothic sandstone spires of Utah's Fisher Towers to the pre-Cambrian granite abysses of Colorado's Black Canyon. It is a state of being I deeply cherish. It keeps me sane in an overly complex, materially driven world, and it is what convinced me leave my native Appalachia and settle in the Four Corners region.

Years later, I would discover that this Angel Peak revelation – a gift of masked dancers, coyotes, and lightning – came to me at the center of the world.

In the 11th century, nearly 400 miles of roads radiated from Chaco Canyon like the rays of a stylized sun. The Chacoans designed these roads for foot travel, and yet some of them reached 20 to 30 feet across. Along them journeyed messengers, priests, warriors, workmen with ponderosa logs for the great multi-storied buildings, and traders with packs loaded with corn, pottery, turquoise, and more exotic products like shells from the Pacific Ocean or parrot feathers from the Mexican realms of the Toltecs and Mayas. The roads were absolutely straight and largely ignored natural contours, moving directly over mesas and across valleys. To some anthropologists, the geometric perfection of these roads suggests that they served important religious and symbolic roles in addition to their practical function of facilitating foot travel across the desert.

Most of the Chacoan roads head south or southwest towards the fertile foothills and canyons west of Mount Taylor, where thousands of farmers grew the grains that kept the Chacoan civilization alive. An exception is the North Road, which begins at Pueblo Alto, at the top of Chaco Canyon across from Casa Rinconada and above Pueblo Bonito. This major route heads directly north and passes through the ruins named El Faro and Halfway House, which both served as way stations and guard towers along the road. After crossing thirty miles of nearly uninhabited territory, the North Road arrives at Kutz Canyon and Angel Peak, where centuries ago it descended a wooden staircase and ended at the canyon floor. For decades, archeologists have assumed that from Kutz Canyon the road continued northwest to reach the Anasazi cities of Salmon and Aztec, but no such extension has ever been discovered.

In his book *Anasazi America*, University of New Mexico archeologist David E. Stuart reveals a conversation he had with Pueblo Indian anthropologist Alfonso Ortiz concerning Chaco's North Road. Stuart complained to Ortiz that the North Road had served no discernable purpose, because even in the 11th century it traveled through a sparsely populated region and ended in a desolate and uninhabited canyon. Ortiz responded to Stuart's assertion by challenging its cultural assumptions. As Stuart describes, "Alfonso smiled enigmatically and suggested that road went nowhere as defined by my world – not by his."

Stuart then explains archeologist Michael Marshall's theory that the Pueblo Indians at Chaco Canyon believed that Kutz Canyon was the place of emergence, the chasm where the first people ascended from the previous world to enter this one. In Pueblo Indian belief, there have been four previous worlds, and each time one was destroyed, the survivors entered the next realm through an opening in the ground, the Sipapu, commemorated by a hole in the earth in many kivas. Today's Pueblo Indians identify many different locales as the emergence point, including the Grand Canyon by the Hopi and Blue Lake in the Sangre de Cristo Mountains by the Indians of Taos Pueblo. Regardless of where a particular tribe believes it to be, it is a place of primary sacredness, the sole entry-point into our new universe – the center of the world.

≈≈≈

Some pilgrims, seeking the geographical center of their faith, journey to Jerusalem. Others, with different beliefs, find their way to Rome, Stonehenge, Delphi, Mecca, Benares,

Lhasa, Tai Shan, Mount Fuji, Mount Kilimanjaro, Ayers Rock, Teotihuacan, or some other storied place, famous in the annals of human history and religion.

By accident, I found my way to a humble canyon at the end of a dirt road barely noted on the official New Mexico state highway map. There, before a spire named for the Christian version of Pueblo Indian kachinas, next to a sacred canyon scarred by natural gas pumps, I encountered a night of masked gods, the holy Trickster, and the blue fire of Quetzalcoatl, the mighty Plumed Serpent of the Toltecs. This encounter opened up my soul to a new reality – a new way to see the world, a new land to call home.

A Canticle of Owls

Bitáhatini, the Visionary, was returning to his home at Tse'gíhi in Dinétah, the land of the Navajos.

He had been gone for nine days in the secret canyon where the Yéi, the Holy People, dwell. There they taught him the dances and songs of the Night Chant, a powerful healing ceremony that would change the lives of the Navajo, the Diné, forever. He felt profoundly grateful for this gift that the Yéi had chosen him to receive.

As he descended the plateau which held the sacred canyon of the Yéi, Bitáhatini passed into a grove of piñon, and the sandstone landscape disappeared behind a dense labyrinth of the scraggly pines. Once he was well within the grove, he heard a deep, resonant call, like the low notes on a large flute. He stopped and looked all around to see who had made the sound, but no one was there. So, he continued on his journey. Again, the call came, and again Bitáhatini peered into the trees and along the path, but saw no one. He once more started to walk, and the call rang out a third time, with the same results. With the fourth call, the Visionary quickly turned and found a great horned owl peering down at him from the highest branch of the eldest piñon.

"Come close, my grandson," bid the owl in a cavernous voice.

Bitáhatini approached the tree until he was staring right into the owl's round, yellow eyes, their pupils as black as the darkness between the stars.

"You have just been to Hastsédespin, the realm of the Yéi, where they taught you the Night Chant."

"Yes."

"There is a thing they have not revealed to you – how to make the yádi-dinil, the incense for the fire. The Yéi, being holy ones, fear what it is made from. But without the yádidinil, the healing will not take place. This is why I have followed you, to teach you how to make the healing smoke."

And the owl proceeded to teach Bitáhatini, the Visionary, the forbidden knowledge of how to make the yádidinil, thus completing the Night Chant and thereby unleashing its healing power.

〰 〰 〰

Through his lonely adventures in the wilderness, Bitáhatini, a prophet of the Diné, brought the sacred healing ceremonies to his people. However, these ceremonies would not have worked without the help of the great-horned owl. Despite this, the Diné, like most Southwestern American Indians, generally view owls with intense suspicion, associating them with illness, death, and witchcraft.

Owls have a powerful place in myths across the planet, representing everything from supermundane wisdom to blasphemous evil. The story of how the Visionary received the Night Chant combines these concepts of the owl, since the forbidden knowledge the owl reveals is absolutely necessary to make the healing ceremonies work, and yet it is so unclean that only the owl can teach it to Bitáhatini.

This dualistic characteristic of owls makes having an association with them an ambiguous boon. In many cultures, a companion to owls is regarded with suspicion, even hostility. For instance, Bitáhatini's brothers thoroughly distrusted him when he returned from the secret canyon of the Yéi, a common reaction to those who associate with owls.

Despite knowing this, I remain a member of the owl fraternity.

〰 〰 〰

I first became aware of my kinship with owls when I was fifteen. It was late March in upstate New York, and a beloved dog, a Border Collie mix named Trixie, had been missing for over a month. One grey, chilly afternoon, I went for a walk through the sycamore grove that grew along the Owego River near my home. I hadn't been by the river in months because of the sheath of jagged ice that all winter had covered its surface and had even reached past its banks into the sycamore swamp. However, the ice had recently thawed and the swamp had drained, so this was my first chance since December to wander through one of my favorite places to explore. While walking through a stony flood basin, I spotted something that made my heart turn cold. There, amidst the debris of dead branches and milkweed stalks, caught on the snag of a fallen log, rested my dog's body – head twisted, teeth in a grimace, its white and tan markings matted, yet unmistakable.

I spent much of that afternoon crying, but by nightfall, I had regained some self-control, though the hurt was just as deep. I was down in the basement workshop helping my father on a woodworking project when he sent me to fetch a rubber mallet from the barn. Before heading outside, I turned on the outdoor floodlights, which illuminated the back yard and threw deep shadows in the starless night. The darkness made me uneasy, so I quickly strode past the willow, entered the barn, snapped on the overhead bulb, and grabbed the hammer from the wood slab bench. Then I closed the side-door to the barn and started back, only to stop by the willow. The floodlight was backlighting the tree, creating a series of concentric circles in the branches. And on the willow's inner branches, framed by the circles of light, there perched a stocky bird, less than a foot high with a large head, rounded wings, a square tail, and pointed ear tufts.

It was a screech owl.

Despite the owl being entirely in silhouette, I could sense it was staring straight at me. I felt chilled, and not from the damp air. After a time, I walked past, and the bird's head turned to follow me. When I was beyond the tree, I glanced back. While its body had remained motionless, its head had turned near-ly all the way round to follow my progress – a very unnerving sight. Now that the floodlight was shining fully on it, I could clearly see its brown-grey body, hooked beak, and large round eyes.

I had never been so close to an owl, and the encounter left me feeling strangely connected to this bird of prey. Later, as I was falling asleep, the death of my dog, while it still hurt, seemed less sharply tragic, and simply a part of the world's natural rhythms of light and shadow.

≈≈≈

A decade later, I had a second encounter with a screech owl in the Blue Ridge Mountains of southwestern Virginia. In those days, I lived in an old farmhouse next to a small, swift-running stream. The county road that connected the main highway to a cluster of backcountry farms had at one time run past the faded clapboard house with its two-story front porch. An abandoned store built from unpainted wood planks stood fifty yards down the way. But decades before, the county road had been straightened, and the old thoroughfare had become a dirt track that reached a dead end at my home.

The house, well over a century old, felt mired in time's deep shadows. My first wife Patricia and I lived in several rooms on the first floor. The rest of the house, including the main parlor on the first floor and the entire second floor, was closed up. Sometimes we would see ghosts in those unused rooms – an old bald-headed man writing at a ledger, a woman in a long grey dress standing at a window, a German shepherd staring from an open door. On warm nights, 1930's swing music would inexplicably drift through the open windows of our bedroom, as if there were a radio in the woodshed out back. And when I entered the old store, I would experience an overwhelming feeling of oppression and despair. Except to store seldom-used tools and glass jugs, I avoided it, day or night.

However, the land around the house possessed a prelapsarian serenity. To the north, a hay field stretched to the road. To the east, a stream cradled the house, its banks covered in scrub willows and flowering rhododendrons. To the south, a forest of maple, ironwood, and pine surrounded the old, barely discernible moss-covered road. And to the west, a steep hill rose with scattered blackberry bushes, walnut trees, and pastureland. At night, in the late spring, tens of thousands of fireflies would cover this hillside, a drifting galaxy of moving lights.

The house faced west, and between it and the hill stood a great oak. On summer days, a pair of black snakes that lived in our woodshed would drape themselves from the lower branches, resting from a busy morning of devouring mice. And at dusk, I would often spot a screech owl perched high enough in the tree to be safe from the snakes. Most days I would be content to peer up at it from the ground, its body rigid and alert in its search for prey. Occasionally, I would stand on the front porch's second level and gaze directly into the owl's eyes. When I would sit on the front lawn watching the fireflies in their deep midnight dance, I would hear the owl's eerie trilling sound, like a soul calling its ancestors.

≈≈≈

When I moved to New Mexico, my connection with owls deepened.

One of my favorite places to hike was a deep, basaltic canyon outside of Santa Fe that the locals called Diablo Canyon, though the National Forest maps name it Caja del Rio Canyon. This canyon rests at the end of Buckman Road, a backcountry route that runs from U.S. 85 to the banks of the Rio Grande. An old railroad bed, it once carried narrow gauge trains on their way from Santa Fe to Antonito, Colorado. Now it is dirt road for Jeeps and pick-up trucks.

One clear June night, there was going to be a nearly full moon, and so I set out to explore the canyon under its pale white light. Back then, I drove a 1969 Toyota Land Cruiser, and about an hour after sunset, I jumped into the boxy red cab, tossed a canteen on the passenger seat, and took off down Buckman Road. As I rolled through sand hills covered in piñon and juniper, the sun's last embers were dying on a western horizon formed from the gentle curves of the Jemez Mountains. Overhead, the stars struggled to shine through a sky awash in the gibbous moon's glow.

After a time, the road straightened to descend the gradual sweep of the Caja del Rio Plateau. Dusty mounds of sagebrush and saltbush had replaced the piñons and junipers. Here and there, a patch of Mormon tea looked like a spiky cloud descended to the earth. Caught in the headlights, deer mice, jackrabbits, and the occasional kangaroo rat scurried away into the dark. Once, the ghost of a coyote slid at the edges of the Land Cruiser's illumination. And every half mile or so, nine-inch burrowing owls – their tan, earless forms tucked beneath camouflaging bushes or overhanging stone slabs – hunted in the half-darkness.

After nearly an hour, I reached the Diablo Canyon fork. I turned left, driving over a rough, rocky road until I stopped at a wide, sandy space on the edge of the dry wash of the Cañada Ancha. Though I could drive down this into the canyon's heart, I decided to walk instead. Getting out, I was blessed with silence, a true delight after the banging and rattling of the old Land Cruiser. Of course, it wasn't completely silent. There were crickets and cicadas singing, and a warm evening breeze sighed through the sage. As I shut the door, it made a hollow, metallic bang in the quiet night. I hadn't brought a flashlight, so I stood for a time to let my eyes adjust to the light of the moon, which was approaching zenith.

Finally, I could make out the road as it cut to the left to reach the floor of the wash, and the high, utterly black cliffs of the canyon entrance ahead. I followed the road into the arroyo and passed into Diablo Canyon. The arroyo bottom was sandy, though here and there basaltic boulders loomed like sleeping bears, and the floor was strewn with round stones that challenged my footing. The walls rose higher about me, great black fortresses of rock. The moonlight illuminated only the canyon's top half. Further down the canyon it was like the interior of a cave – dark, impenetrable, unknowable. I began to hear scurrying in the brush near the canyon walls, and becoming uneasy, I halted. However, the shifting creatures also stopped. Outside of my breathing, all was quiet.

And then it drifted down from the highest cliffs – the call of a great horned owl – low and pure, like the tones from an Indian flute.

An owl across the dark canyon's divide picked up the call.

At my back, a third joined in.

Thus, I stood there in the haunted night as the owls spoke of deep mysteries – of death, metamorphosis, and regeneration. I heard no more movement, for now the prey had become fearful. And yet, strange to say, I felt peaceful, protected. My owls were there, watching over my journey into the shadow lands.

≈≈≈

Despite the sometimes dark and disturbing associations they can evoke, owls are amazing creatures.

According to Tony Angell in his outstanding book, *The House of Owls*, there are over 200 species of owls – ranging from the little six-inch elf owl that lives in the saguaro cactus of the Sonoran Desert to the mighty Blakiston's fish owl of Siberia, which has a six-foot wingspan. Most species of owl have comb-like serrated feathers with uneven edges. This allows them to fly in nearly total silence as they perform their nocturnal hunting. The sight of a moonlit owl diving soundlessly from the shadows of a looming stone bluff or the shadowy bulk of an ash tree to slay a hapless rabbit probably inspired the widespread belief that the owl is a bird of death and evil.

And yet, with its disk face and forward facing, narrow-set eyes, the owl bears the greatest resemblance to humans of all avian species. Like a dish antenna, this flat, circular face is a remarkable focus for sound and light, contributing to the owl's keen sense of hearing and sight. For instance, a boreal owl in flight can not only detect the sounds of a vole moving under a deep layer of snow, but use those sounds to capture its well-hidden, diminutive prey. Owls communicate through sets of complex tones, and they can be surprisingly gregarious, sharing food with nest mates and forming widely dispersed yet interconnected communities.

With such human characteristics, it's no surprise that the owl has a prominent role in world mythology.

According to Marija Gimbutas, an archeologist who specialized in ancient Europe, humans have been carving sacred images of owls since 13,000 BCE. A cave called the Gallery of Owls holds the oldest known depictions of this bird of prey – three snowy owls engraved on a limestone ceiling.

Later, in the Neolithic Era, when Europeans developed farming and built their first cities, the owl represented the death aspect of the Great Goddess, with all the attendant wisdom that comes with old age and the transition into the next world. Clay images of the owl goddess appear as early as the 8th millennium BCE, and from then until the early Bronze Age, sculptors, potters, and painters depicted her with snakes, vulvas, and labyrinths – indicating that the Neolithic priesthood associated the owl with death, regeneration, and rebirth.

In the middle Bronze Age, around 2,000 BCE, the owl appears again as the death deity in the Mesopotamian goddess Nin-ninna, the "Divine Lady Owl." Later, the Akkadians would call her Kilili, from which the Hebrews derived the figure of Lilith, whose name literally translates into "screech owl." Kilili evolved into the Aegean goddess Athena, the deity of wisdom who was born from the forehead of Zeus, king of the Olympians. The 8th century BCE poet Hesiod described Athena as "the equal of her father in might and good counsel," and her association with the owl deepened its connection with the intellect. However, the owl was still a harbinger of death, since Athena was also a goddess of war. Paul A. Johnsgard, in *North American Owls*, notes that the Athenians believed that Athena, in the form of an owl, led them to their glorious victory over the Persians at Marathon.

As the Greek civilization gave way to the Roman, the association of the owl with death became ascendant. By imperial times, the owl foretold the illness and death of a loved one. The early Christians denigrated the owl even further, viewing the owl as a satanic creature, a seeker of false knowledge, and a devourer of unwary souls. Still, the fertility connotation continued under the owl's dark guise, so that in Welch folklore the hooting of an owl announces a maiden's first sexual experience, and in the south of France the shrieking of a barn owl foretells the birth of a female child.

In the Americas, owls have also encompassed a range of mythological concepts.

For the Cherokee, the owl is a powerful ally, a bringer of wisdom and the nighttime guardian of the tribe's children. The Pawnees also view the owl as a protector of the people, and they decorate the ceremonial pipe of their Hako ritual with owl feathers, while the Hidatsa view the owl as the deity of the game, especially the buffalo. Calling the borrowing owl "priest of the prairie dog," the Zuni give it a role in guiding the creatures of the earth. The Hopi identify the owl with Masau'u – lord of the underworld, protector of the clans, keeper of the sacred fires, and germinator of seeds. The Mayan also connect the owl with fertility, associating the screech owl with clouds, rain, mist, and the coming of maize.

However, other tribes have a more sinister role for the owl. The Pueblo Indians along the Rio Grande and the Navajo of northern Arizona associate the owl with death and witchcraft, as did the Aztec, who called their shape-shifting sorcerers *tlacatecolotl*, or owl man. For the Oto-Missouri and Pima peoples, the owl is an unmistakable manifestation of death, and the Kwakiutl Indians believe that the spirits of the dead make their way to the afterlife by crossing the owl-bridge.

Regardless of its conflicted mythology, or perhaps because of it, I have grown to accept my deep connection with owls, and so they continue to enter my world – a nesting screech owl in a neighbor's mulberry tree, a great horned owl perched motionless in a desert juniper at dusk, the white flash of a barn owl diving across the three-a.m. desert highway. I know they are out there, protecting me, warning me, leading me through their secret passageways into the labyrinthine realm of dreams.

≈≈≈

One late October, nearly three decades ago, I awoke, stiff and cold, from a night of camping south of the Zuni Pueblo, near Largo Mangas Creek. I had slept on a thin foam mattress in the camper shell of my white Toyota pick-up, wrapped up in a dusty-green army surplus sleeping bag. I lay there for some time in the dawn's half-light, staring up at the grooves in the corrugated aluminum roof, feeling the frosty air sting my nose and face, waiting for the sun to rise and warm things up. It seemed to be holding itself back, as if refusing to make an appearance above the low bluffs to the east. Growing impatient, I finally peeled back the sleeping bag. The frigid world shocked my half naked body. Hastily, I pulled on jeans, a heavy flannel shirt, and a blue-jean jacket. This helped, but I was still shivering. Reaching for my plastic jug of water, I discovered it was frozen solid. I set it down with a curse, opened the two horizontal halves of the back door, and slid out.

The valley of the Largo Mangas was even colder than the camper shell. Still, the nearly-risen sun's blaze obscured the eastern bluffs in a hazy glow, and that heartened me. To the west, a high plateau was mired in deep shadow, but its summit blazed like an island on fire. The scattered piñon and juniper on its highest slopes were incredibly sharp in the clear air. Overhead, the sky was pure azure.

I studied the ashes of the previous night's campfire, thought about starting a new one, and rejected the idea. In order to make coffee, much less cook anything, I would have to somehow break the ice in the jug or in my metal canteen in the cab, and it seemed like too much work, especially since I figured I could get breakfast somewhere on US 60. So, after stirring the ashes to make certain they were truly dead, I got behind the wheel, started the truck, and taking one last look at my scrubby campsite, trundled down the rough track to the dirt road that would take me to pavement and civilization.

The dirt road was surprisingly smooth, and I pushed the truck up to 40 mph. Abruptly, in desert fashion, the sun rose, filling the entire valley with light, setting off sparks in the creek's ripples and flashes from the sandstone slabs at the base of the western bluffs. In about a half hour I reached US 60, a highway I had never taken before. Its smooth and flawless surface rolled from east to west like a blacktop ribbon to the infinite.

I turned left. Like a strange dream, the bright world shot by at sixty-five miles per hour. Soon I reached a cluster of clapboard houses and trailers called Quemado. There, I pulled into the lot for a rough, wood-frame structure that served as a roadside diner. Inside, at a fifteen-foot counter, three seats away from a stocky, silent man in a dirt-stained cowboy hat, I had buttermilk pancakes with maple-flavored syrup and strong, bitter coffee.

Back on the road, I shot between desert mountains through a series of small towns much like Quemado. First there came Omega and Pie Town, and then after the stone walls of White House Canyon, Datil. Just past Datil, a two-decade old flatbed truck with a red cab passed me in the other direction, and then the land opened out in a vast prairie ringed by distant mountains.

These were the Plains of San Agustin.

In my pick-up, I felt like a diminutive insect scurrying across that immense space. The speedometer read seventy miles per hour, but it seemed as if I were making no progress along the absolutely straight highway. I felt like a ray of light attempting to reach the universe's far edge. Yet, as the sun angled higher, the flat expanse of brush and grass did roll past, and the distant mountains to the east grew closer and more distinct.

About a third of the way across the plains, a vision from a future century loomed into view. A row of maybe fifty radio telescopes stretched off in a line to the southwest. Their identical white dishes, each with a black radio tower in the center like pistils in a row of immense metal flowers, receded with mechanical precision towards the prairie's far rim.

This was the Very Large Array – a set of radio telescopes that work as one, thereby replicating a single structure 20 miles in diameter. All the dishes were raised forty-five degrees and facing the southeast, taking in the signals from some invisible object in the pale blue sky.

When I reached the salt flats, I slowed so I could study this strange new sight. I had read about the VLA, and I had expected to see it on the way back home to Santa Fe, but I had not been prepared for the wonder of this fabulous assemblage of antennae arrowing off towards the mountains like giant sentinels. The resulting scene possessed all the surreal attributes of a science-fiction movie.

Finally, where the line of radio telescopes intersects the highway, I could make out the control center – a low white building with a scattering of windows across its exterior and a few autos parked in its shade. Suddenly, the whole apparition slid beyond the view of my passenger-side window.

Looking back at the highway, I started picking up speed when an object just past the road's left shoulder caught my eye. It was a brown lump, maybe the size of a spaniel. Normally I would have kept on going, but the wind lifted something that looked like a wing, so I slowed and made a U-turn. I pulled up beside the object and got out of the truck.

It was a great-horned owl.

Longer than my forearm, the deceased owl lay on its side, one wing underneath, the other facing me. As the wind blew dust in my tearing eyes, the free wing would rise, giving the signal that had brought me to it. The great yellow eyes were closed, as was the hooked beak. I placed my hand on its massive side. The body was still warm. It must have died within the previous few hours, dawn at the latest. Since there was no blood, I guessed that the owl had flown into a vehicle's windshield where there were no edges to cause punctures. I remembered the flat-bed truck I had just passed near Datil. Perhaps it had been the destroyer.

I squatted that way for some ten minutes, my hand placed on the owl's body, studying the fine pattern of its brown and beige feathers; the round, noble face with its disturbing beak and tufts of pale down; the solid, almost stout frame. Now and then I would peer up at the salt flats, the prairie, and the low mountains beyond.

At last, I stood and went for my entrenching tool. I reached into the back of the truck and pulled out the small, quarter-sized shovel I had picked up in a Flagstaff army surplus store. Before closing the camper-shell door, I glanced over at the radio telescopes. They were still pointing southeast at their 45-degree angle.

Returning to the owl, I began the dig. The ground, topped by a thin layer of light grey, alkaline soil, was sandy and easy to turn. When the hole reached its proper size, I placed the owl in, still on its side. While I shoveled the cinnamon-colored earth to cover it, I heard a medium-pitched whirring sound from behind me, like the spinning of an electrically powered machine.

Standing, I turned and looked across the road. All the antennae of the Very Large Array were turning in graceful unison, silent except for the whirring sound of their motors, a magnetically induced canticle nearly masked by the light breeze. They moved with stately precision, a ballet of gears and pulleys and enormous white discs. Within moments they ceased. All the antennae now faced at a point above the western horizon, again at some invisible object – a star, a quasar, a pulsar, a nebula – well beyond heaven's blue dome. It was as if the array had tracked the owl's soul, released by the burial to begin a sojourn across the solar system and into interstellar space.

Once the antennae ceased their turning, I finished burying the owl and returned to my truck. I sat for a time studying the road, meditating on what had just taken place. It seemed to me then, and seems to me now, that this witnessing of the many antennae of the Very Large Array shifting with the owl's burial was the culminating sign of my connection with this fascinating and mythologically empowered bird of prey – keeper of dreams, bringer of wisdom, the totem of Athena.

Finally, as the Magdalena Mountains before me grew brighter, the weight of all the hundreds of miles I needed to cover before reaching home broke into my contemplations.

So, starting the truck, I headed east, towards the sun.

Coyote's Road

(O)ur journey to the underworld had its origins one sunny fall day on the northern Arizona highlands.

My two daughters and I were exploring Sunset Crater National Monument, the site of a volcanic cinder cone that formed in 1065 C.E., a mere eye-blink ago in geological time. The cone is beautifully dark and symmetrical, and the dramatically violent eruption that formed it also shaped the region's elder mythology. We were taking a trail that meanders through the congealed lava flow along the cone's base, a place of strangely twisted rock, tortured by wind and frost, filled with holes and broken gas bubbles. Along this trail, at the bottom of a small pit formed from collapsed rubble, we came to the opening of a lava tube – a cave formed when molten lava flows through an already cooled and hardened crust. The Park Service had blocked this particular tube because it had become unstable, but the trail guide noted that the Lava River Cave, about fifty miles west in the San Francisco Mountain foothills, was open to the public. Though it was formed 700,000 years before Sunset Crater, the trail guide assured that the cave was intact and safe for travel.

As we looked past the iron grate blocking off the lava tube's entrance and into the shadowy interior beyond, we promised ourselves that we would someday descend into Lava River Cave.

A year later we are fulfilling our vow.

~~~

After driving along a rutted dirt road through forests of dusty green pine and the occasional darker spruce, we park alongside about a dozen cars and begin walking along a wide trail. Ursula, my oldest daughter, is tall and slender, with dark blond hair reaching straight past her back's mid-point. She is an English major at Colorado Mesa University, and a writer of fanciful tales filled with witches and faeries, runes and ancient tombs. Two years younger, Isadora, a chemistry major at Northern Arizona University, works instead in the realm glass retorts, beakers, and flasks. She is a slight, elfin figure with severely cut light blond hair. Both wear black coats that nearly reach their knees.

A stiff wind causes the pines to sigh, and the autumnal sun blazes past shifting needles. Passing a family heading back to their car, we notice that everyone's gaze seems distant and disturbed, as if focused on a mysterious planet hovering on the horizon. A little girl of about seven says to her father, "That was awful. I never want to do that again." It makes me wonder what awaits us.

Soon after, much more quickly than we anticipated, we reach an open circle formed by a low wall of basaltic stones. The circle is about ten yards in diameter and reminds me of the Pueblo Indian kivas one finds in their ruined cities. Entering the ring, we climb down a slope of stone rubble to a rough oval opening in the ground. Ahead of us, two people with dark blue wool plaid jackets vanish into the opening. We follow.

Inside, the broken slope continues downward. As we carefully make our way into the earth, the light rapidly fades. We pass to the left of a stone pillar and turn on our flashlights. The ground beneath our feet is uncertain. Some of the head-sized stones shift and wobble under our tread. Ahead of us, the blue plaid couple, along with their flashlights, silently vanish as if swallowed whole by a massive black snake.

In ten minutes we reach the cave's floor. Up the slope behind us, the jagged oval entrance glows with a diminished light that disappears altogether when we enter the cave's serpentine curves. Isadora leads. Ursula, the one without a flashlight, comes next, and I bring up the rear, lighting a path for both my oldest daughter and me. Mostly, we keep our lights on the floor because we are traversing great slabs of rock broken into irregular rectangles and triangles that can trick the feet. One rift between slabs causes Ursula to stumble, and when she grabs her sister for support, Isadora's light wavers and jumps from the impact. But further along the stone channel, the floor becomes nearly flat, with an odd, bumpy texture. Here and there, small pools reflect our lights, the result of ground water dripping through the stone ceiling. The air is cool, musty, and damp.

Occasionally we stop and shine our electric torches up to see intricate patterns of white and silver colored mineral deposits or tiny mounds of stone like infant stalactites, formed when the final subterranean blasts partially melted the ceiling.

The lava tube is very different from any cave I have explored. Except for the floor, it possesses a smooth, oval shape, as if a great and powerful serpent had bored its way through the volcanic flow. And yet the size keeps changing. At times, the passage is tight. Two or three people with arms outstretched could span the width, and the ceiling is so low we have to hunch over to pass. At other moments, the cave opens out into sweeping arched chambers forty or fifty feet high. Usually after straight stretches, the lava tube tightly coils, almost doubling back on itself.

Because of these coils, we are often alone, our two small lights the only illumination. But now and then, especially in the large chambers, we encounter people heading back out, their lights first appearing far off like tiny wandering stars lost in a vast dark nebula. Where the cave does bend sharply, their forms seemingly materialize out of a nearby stone wall. In the cave, voices become oddly jumbled, and it is difficult to make out what people are saying. More than once, what I think is Russian or French ultimately resolves into English. When meeting these other explorers, there is a mingling of lights which illuminates much of the cave. But after the strangers drift away, we are left with our two modest torches and the deep darkness.

In one long, straight tunnel, we find a tongue of lava hardened into a series of waves, another effect, like the bumpy ceiling, of the lava flow's final inferno. The waves give way to a hump extending along the cave's floor like the spine of a whiptail lizard. But this spine has a fissure, for when the lava stream cooled, it cracked, the way a loaf of bread cracks as it rises in the oven. We follow the fissure for about a hundred yards until it sinks into the floor of a high, spherical cavity. At the cavity's end, two openings about the size of a picture window lead deeper into the underworld.

"Which one is the main tunnel?" Isadora asks in her high, piping voice.

"I have no idea," I answer.

"They might both continue for quite a distance. Or, one could quickly dead end," Ursula says, her words muffled by the dark stone walls.

"The right one has a broader, clearer floor," observes Isadora.

"Yes," Ursula responds. "But it seems to lead upward. Don't we want to go deeper?"

"Whichever one we take, we'll need to keep track of our choice so we don't get lost," I caution.

We send our pathetic light beams into each channel, but both disappear into labyrinthine curves, revealing nothing. I feel like Professor Hardwigg facing a fork in his subterranean route beneath Mount Sneffels in Jules Verne's *Journey to the Center of the Earth*. Which direction should we take? We study each passage in turn. The left tunnel heads slightly downward, but its floor is covered in small slabs of stone rubble. As Ursula said, the right one rises slightly, but it is smooth floored and runs a greater distance before curving out of sight. Just when we decide to take the right passage, a woman's voice calls out behind us, from the spherical chamber's far side.

"Take the left tube. The right one quickly closes off."

Startled, we look behind. No lights. Our oracle must have ducked out of sight past a major curve immediately after giving us her advice.

Heeding the mysterious voice, we plunge into the left channel, our boots alternately crunching on crumbling stone, slapping on smooth lava, or whispering on a bumpy surface. More twists and bends. The cave narrows and opens, narrows again. The narrowing increases.

We turn into another spherical room, much smaller than the one at the fork, and stop short. Here, the passage beyond becomes an eye-shaped slit. We would have to crawl if we want to proceed.

"We should head back," I announce in the silence, my flashlight focused on the narrow opening.

"Yeah," Ursula agrees. "I don't feel like making my way through such a small space."

"Ok," Isadora adds. "But before we go, let's do something. Remember when we were in that cave by Glenwood Springs, and the guide turned off all the lights? That was really cool."

"And you want to do that now?" I ask.

"Yes."

"Ursula, is that all right with you?"

After a pause, Ursula assents. Isadora and I turn off our flashlights.

≈≈≈

The cave is absolutely black.

"It's like being in a room at midnight with the lights off and the shutters closed," Ursula says quietly.

"No," Isadora declares. "It's far beyond even that."

I wave my right hand, the one clutching the flashlight, in front of my face.

I see only total darkness. No hand. No arm. No flashlight.

Minutes pass, and I see a phosphorescent blotch to my left. I think it is on the cave wall, but when I turn, it is not there. It is an illusion, a mental reaction to the total absence of light.

As more time slides away, the darkness stirs my imagination. I drop into the deep unconscious, realm of the gods, and begin to have visions.

Hades, the Greek underworld, is the first image to arise.

In southern Greece, near Diros Bay, there is a vast cavern named Alepotrypa. In ancient mythological tradition, it is the opening to Hades, the realm of the dead. I have never been there, but I imagine it possesses the same untarnished darkness I am experiencing here in Lava River Cave. In Greek pagan belief, when you die, Hermes, the crosser of boundaries, guides your soul down Alepotrypa Cavern to the River Styx. There, you pay Charon, the boatman, to ferry you across. Beyond the Styx, you walk past Cerberus, the three-headed dog who guards Hades. Finally, after the uncompromising gaze of Cerberus, you reach a vaulted chamber where the three judges of the dead – Minos, Rhadamthys, and Aeacus – determine the decades you will dwell in Elysium in reward for your good deeds, and the decades you will endure the hellscape of Tartarus in punishment for your sins. After a thousand years interned in the underworld, you are reborn.

The inner portrait of Hades dissolves, replaced by the Labyrinth of Crete and Theseus' pursuit of the Minotaur through winding, oval passages of stone, a smoky torch his only light.

After slaying the Minotaur, Theseus hands the torch to Masau'u – Hopi god of the dead, guide of souls, guardian of the Fourth World, horned personage of smoke and fire. Like Hermes, he too is a trickster. He leads me down into the Grand Canyon, where we enter an opening carved in a high cliff's basaltic roots. Inside, we traverse a long, granite tunnel and arrive at a vast domed cavity, its stone ceiling so high I feel like I am outdoors on a cloudy evening. Here, Masau'u leads me across the plaza of an immense pueblo, seven stories high, greater than any Indian village I have ever seen, living or dead. A dull red light permeates the scene, and I dimly make out men and women in Hopi kirtles moving quietly through the gloom, grinding corn and tanning hides. Upon leaving the pueblo, we enter another tunnel, and at its end we surface into a small desert canyon. It is night, and overhead the stars blaze in multitudinous glory. I follow the horned god and emerge from the canyon near a carnival on the edge of Kayenta, a crossroads town on the Navajo reservation. Standing amidst the spinning rockets and

Ouroboros merry-go-round, Masau'u faces me and points to the Ferris wheel, its struts outlined in purple and green LED lights, as pure and bright as lasers. The wheel turns, illuminating a coyote heading south along a dirt road. I follow the coyote to an arroyo where autumnal cottonwoods drop their golden leaves under a dying half-moon. There, the coyote confronts me. Its eyes, lit by moonlight, have a wild, untamed gaze.

The coyote unnerves me, and I turn on my flashlight. Isadora does the same. Their twined beams are an enormous relief. We decide to begin our long journey back to the half-forgotten daylight world outside.

≈≈≈

I am not used to hiking underground, and though the rust-red walls slip steadily behind us, the return trek feels longer. Also, I keep imagining that we are heading along a different cave, because our twin cones of light reveal features unlike those we saw on our way in. As I grow anxious, my mind again wanders on disturbing paths. The ash-colored patches of stone remind me of a certain cave I once explored at the base of El Cuchillo del Medio, a craggy-faced mountain in northern New Mexico. This cave has ragged, limestone walls and does not burrow as deeply as Lava River Cave, but it is still a place of disturbing power. In *Mountain Dialogues*, southwestern author Frank Waters, who lived at the base of El Cuchillo, reports the local rumors that the cave is a meeting place for witches, and that the Pueblo Indians in pre-colonial times used it for human sacrifice. For D.H. Lawrence, who visited the cave when he lived on his Taos ranch, it became the setting for an Indian sacrifice of a wealthy American woman in his novella "The Woman Who Rode Away." And while Lava River Cave does not feel evil, like the cave in El Cuchillo, it is still an opening to the dark underworld with its hidden universe of repressed memories and negative archetypes.

"I wonder if the Hopi ever came down here?" Isadora asks. I am a bit startled that she too has Pueblo Indian mythology on her mind.

"It's hard to say," I respond, my voice oddly dampened by the dead, damp, cool air. "I don't believe anyone has ever found any cultural artifacts down here – objects like pottery, prayer sticks, or petroglyphs – that would confirm the Hopi had explored these lava tubes. Still, one would think that either the Hopi or the pre-Columbian Sinagua, who lived by Sunset Crater, would have found the entrance and made the descent."

"Are the Pueblo Indians all one tribe?"

"No," I reply, explaining that although there are a great many similarities between the Pueblo peoples, there are six distinct tribes, each with their own language and culture. I recite the groups, and each name marks another step in the dark passage:

Hopi

Zuni

Tewa

Tiwa

Towa

and Keres.

"Also, there once were the Hano," I finish. "They died out in the early 19th century from diseases brought by the European colonists." With this, my voice ceases, and the black silence settles in around us, as if remembering the long vanished Hano.

≈≈≈

Distended minutes weave our passage through the rock, and at last we reach the base of the slope that leads to the opening. To our surprise, there are almost a dozen people waiting to climb to the ragged hole of blue-white light because, about half-way up, near the stone pillar that divides the passage, an elderly woman in a red parka struggles with the steep rubble covered incline. A younger man, perhaps her son, has hold of her arm, trying to help her. My daughters and I turn off our lights, and I am fascinated by how dark it still is even though the cave opening is within our sight. It's like being in a canyon of charcoal colored granite lit only by a crescent moon. We watch as the parka-clad woman keeps sliding in failure. Finally, nearly carried by her son, she reaches the entrance and disappears through it. The others start up, and after maybe ten minutes, it is our turn.

Our flashlights snap back on, pushing the shadows away from the path. The rocks feel uncertain, and the grade more challenging than before. When we reach the pillar, the glow from the outside becomes strong enough that we can pick up our pace. Rising through the mouth of the earth, we return to the stone circle, the open air, and the life-giving sun. Everything is bright and sharply defined, almost hallucinogenic. The ponderosa pines flash in the afternoon's solar fire. I can see every cluster of green needles, every crack in the rough reddish-brown bark. The air is alive with the smell of pines; the sky is an infinite blue. In the Hopi emergence myth, the people who have remained true to the Sun Father's ways survive the icy destruction of the Second World by hiding in a great anthill. When the Third World is ready, Sótuknang, the Sun's nephew, bids the people to climb out of the anthill. Leaving the lava tube, I feel that I too have climbed into the warm light of a newly created planet.

On the trail back to the car, a grinning Isadora expresses her delight in our underground expedition. "We should do this again," she says. "But next time let's bring better flashlights."

"No thank-you," Ursula says in her deeper toned voice.

Glancing over, I notice that her round face is frowning, the brows depressed, her blue gaze troubled.

"Are you all right?" I ask.

"No. Not really."

She falls silent. The wind ceases. The pines stop their song.

"What's wrong?"

Ursula wraps her arms just under her breasts, as if trying to keep warm, even though the sunlight is pleasantly strong.

"The cave. I could feel the dead in there."

"The dead?"

"Souls. Souls of the dead." She stumbles on a stone in the trail, catches her balance, and keeps going. "No. I am never returning to the cave."

Isadora, a scientist to her core, shakes her head and sighs. But I wonder, were there spirits in the dark? I try to recall the moment when we turned off the flashlights and stood in total darkness. What did I experience? Why did I become uneasy? But all I can fully remember is the trickster coyote heading down the road in the light of the Navajo fair's Ferris wheel.

In *The Republic*, Plato relates the story of Er, a soldier who was left for dead on a battlefield, journeyed to Hades for twelve days, and was allowed to return so that humanity could learn the truth of what lies beyond the River Styx. According to Er, we have all died and been reborn many times, each death a thousand-year sojourn. Just before we are reborn, we drink from the River Lethe, its waters washing away all memory of the millennia we have spent in the realm of the dead.

If the ancient Greeks were right, I have drunk from the River Lethe many, many times. Thus, the unnerving memory of Tartarus' absolute darkness, where all the lights are extinguished, fades. Again and again, Hermes, the trickster god, or perhaps his Hopi manifestation Masau'u, has lead me to the cave of the underworld upon my death. I know I will repeat this journey a thousand, thousand times.

And as always, coyote waits, his form gliding down the soul's final road in the carnival night.

The Gates of Eden

Autumn had arrived in western Colorado, the summer's heat had fled, and it was time for my annual pilgrimage to Dominquez Canyon, with its high sandstone cliffs, wind-carved rock towers, and perpetual waters pouring over quartz infused granite formed when the planet was young. Since Dominquez Canyon is one of my favorite destinations, I would usually round up my entire family to hike there with me. But on this October morning, Isadora, my youngest daughter, was off to graduate school in New Mexico; Ursula, her sister, was visiting her mother across town; and my wife Brenda, a professor of sociology, had a set of papers she simply had to grade or her students would be "beating down her office door on Monday."

So, on that nearly cloudless blue day, I alone left the city of Grand Junction, crossed the lower shelf of the Grand Mesa, and turned down Deer Creek Gulch through shale hills like red and beige layered stupas rising from the deep earth. Reaching the dirt parking area next to the Union Pacific tracks, I grabbed my daypack, exited the car, and crossed through the white steel gate past the mysterious train signal box, its radio antenna looking like the ray gun cannon from the 1956 movie *Forbidden Planet*. To my right, the Gunnison River flowed northward behind a screen of tamarisk, sage, rabbit brush, and Mormon tea.

Beyond the gate, a dirt road runs between the cliff wall and two sets of tracks that curve along the river's horseshoe bend. The main line is made from the new high-speed welded track – two smooth, continuous ribbons of steel heading off seemingly into infinity. The other line is the siding, an old-style track with finite lengths of rail bolted together by braces and spiked into creosote soaked ties. This siding is named Bridgeport, a place for the trains heading to the Elk Mountain coal mines to pull over and let the loaded trains slide on by to Grand Junction.

After leaving the cliffs and crossing the tracks, the dirt road edges ever closer to the river through a corridor of tamarisk and saltbush. Near the crossing, on a smooth cliff face, someone decades ago had carefully painted "Zuni, N.M." in three-foot-high white letters. This graphic declaration was probably created by a Zuni Indian, one of the many who worked the rails mid-century, back when the Denver & Rio Grande owned the line.

On the other side of the river, a ranch spreads out across the cottonwood groves and pastureland between the flowing waters and the first cliffs of the Uncompahgre Plateau. That day I could hear country music, tinny and distant, floating across the canyon from the small, white-clapboard ranch house. Occasionally, the sound of neighing horses would harmonize with the singers.

Where the road meets the river, two bridges cross the Gunnison. The first bridge is owned by the rancher. With its suspension cables and sagging plank roadway, it looks like something out of a pulp novel. Before the Bureau of Land Management built the second bridge, I used to trespass on this one to get to Dominquez Canyon. At about the middle, with the planks bending beneath my feet, the ranch house would come into view, and I would always imagine the bead of a rifle trained on my torso, bringing on a sharp pang of fear and guilt.

But now, there is a new bridge on federal land so hikers don't need to trespass. This bridge is made of rust-colored steel girders, and makes a clean, professionally engineered line over the river. While it doesn't feel nearly as adventurous as the rancher's bridge, I appreciate no longer transgressing on private property to reach the canyon. Looking down at the river from the bridge, I could see it was running strong, its water soapy and green with silt from recent rains.

After the bridge, I turned left onto an old, rutted ranch road, next to an abandoned canal that had decades ago irrigated the ranch's orchards. Beyond the massive cottonwoods lining the canal, the rust-red sandstone cliffs rose several hundred feet into the white-streaked blue sky. Mountain sheep sometimes perch on the cliffs' sharp-angled stone faces and sneer at the plodding humans below.

But on that day the cliffs were empty of rams guarding their ewes. Instead, I passed several families returning from Dominquez Canyon. In one, a grinning ten-year-old with a buzz cut carried a head-sized piece of black granite, his prize from a long journey. In another, two girls flanked their young parents. The elder girl, her long brown hair in a ponytail, strode with the confidence of an early teen. Her sister, easily five years younger, possessed tightly curled blond hair and bib overalls. The proud owner of toy red binoculars, she would walk five or six paces and then stop to study her surroundings through them. Each time she did this, her mother would shoo her along, and the little girl would pout. Seeing this family, I inevitably thought back to when my daughters were young, and I felt momentarily saddened, wishing they were with me on this hike.

At the canal's end, the trail takes a right turn at a massive boulder, near where the Dominquez Creek meets the Gunnison River. Between this boulder and the river, amidst the salt bush and sage, a scattering of nylon tents formed bright bubbles of yellow, green, and red. Nearby, a gaggle of beached canoes rested from the day's run.

Past the boulder, I approached the Dominquez Creek's lower falls, a ten-foot-wide plunge over a silted-in concrete dam. This cascade has sliced a deep cut through the dark granite shelf that rises like the back of a grey whale, its surface smoothed by streams that flowed before the first Minoan ships set forth from Crete.

Parallel to the falls, about ten yards from them, the trail passes through a gate formed from a moveable section of a wire fence. Crossing through the gate, I entered the wondrous realm of Dominquez Canyon. The trail rolls through sage and scrub between high sandstone cliffs and groves of cottonwoods which line a stream that carves through the canyon's dark granite foundation. Beyond a corral and cattle chute made from splintering wood planks, the canyon makes a sharp curve to the left. Past this bend, I trod over a wide quartz vein churned and eroded by flash floods, its gravel-sized crystals flashing in the sun like strewn diamonds. It was now well past noon, and the day was growing warmer. The occasional travelers heading back towards the Gunnison River were down to their shirtsleeves, their hiking boots raising dust as they struck the earth. Clearly affected by the heat, they would greet me with tired waves and sweaty faces. I found it odd that I encountered no more families. Usually on a Saturday the trail was loaded with children.

Just after the field of quartz, I reached the Dominquez Canyon divide. Straight ahead ran the south canyon with the Little Dominquez Creek, and to the right, the Big Dominquez Creek had formed its own red-rock gorge. In both, sandstone towers rose, some with the eroded holes called window rocks, and some with massive stone faces, carved by wind and rain, their high cheekbones and sharp noses evoking Paleolithic shaman. Normally, I would enter the western canyon, since it holds one of my favorite places in the American Southwest – a maze of smooth, rounded channels in stream-carved granite that end in a fifty-foot waterfall. But most Dominquez Canyon hikers head up the west passage, and I desired solitude. So I took the south trail, which leads downhill past scrub and boulders and crosses the west branch of the Dominquez Creek. Pushing through stunted willows, I traversed the narrow creek by taking three hops on partially submerged rocks, my left boot sliding into the cold water at the third stone.

Here, I again faced a forked trail. One headed downstream to meet up with the south canyon trail. The other, rarely taken, entered the deep granite gorge that lead to the pool formed by the Big Dominquez Creek's upper water-falls. This is the trail I followed, and soon sixty-foot walls of two-billion-year-old Precambrian granite surrounded me. At one point I stopped and placed my palm against the grey, vertical cliff. It was smooth and cool to the touch. This stone was so ancient it was formed when the solar system was half its present age.

Just before the gorge narrowed, I came to a place where a pile of boulders formed a rough wall around a natural garden of cacti, grasses, and blue cornflow-ers. I sat on one of the boulders, watching the stream as it ran over the rocks, studying the sunlight passing through the golden cottonwood leaves. Shimmering spider web strands, several feet long, floated and twisted in the air. Fat dragonflies buzzed above the flowing waters.

I was tempted to end my hike and stay in this paradise, but as the shad-ows from the trees lengthened, an urge to take full advantage of the daylight made me restless, and I decided instead to go deeper into the gorge. Soon the stone walls closed in, the shadows swallowed the stream, and I had to force my way through tangles of willows. The trail finally gave out at a set of tight cliffs that looked like stacked granite cubes fused by quartzite strata. To go further, I would have to wade in the stream. Reluctant to do this, I decided to end my hike there.

I stood for a time, resting, studying the dark cliffs and the blue sky. Finally, I looked in the willows beside me. There, tightly woven into a tripod of tiny branches, a perfectly formed warbler nest caught my attention. It was grey with age, but still beautifully circular like a well-crafted ceramic cup. It had once been a place of life, sheltering green speckled eggs and then tiny chicks hatching into the light, the air. Protected by the willow branches and the high granite walls, that nest had been the entire universe for those newborn warblers, a realm of knitted grasses, mysterious winds, and the warm bodies of their parents. And seeing that perfection, in a canyon on the northeastern edge of the Uncompahgre

Plateau, inevitably stirred memories from when my daughters were very young and viewed their world as a paradise.

≈≈≈

Back in the days when I was still married to their mother, we would take Ursula and Isadora up onto the Uncompahgre Plateau to swim in the headwaters of the Escalante Creek, above where the stream branches at a place called Escalante Forks. A century ago, Escalante Forks was the site of a bustling town with saloons, tanneries, general stores, and a post office, but now there are only fields, ponderosa pines, and scattered ranch houses. We would drive past the private holdings and onto BLM land, where the creek carves through granite blocks five to ten feet high – a miniature echo of the deep gorge where I was now standing studying a warbler's flawless nest twenty miles away.

There, the girls, four and six years old, would strip down to the bathing suits they wore under their shorts and t-shirts, and enter the shallow pools between the granite rocks, where the creek's clean, flawless water would rest from the diminutive waterfalls upstream. Their mother and I would sit on the rocks and watch as they played, two blond sprites exploring the banks, the tiny stone islands, the sparkling ripples. Sometimes they would release twigs into the current and follow their progress through the miniscule canyon. Other days they would search for crayfish and minnows, or build dams in side channels with stones and mud that quickly dried in the hot sun. Once, a tarantula crawled along the rocks, a strange shadow creature in this Garden of Eden. Thus, Escalante Forks became a microcosm of their wondrous childhood.

And then, the Archangel Michael arrived, his flaming sword raised above the land.

Instead of flowing waters, dark junipers, and towering pines, picture a 1920's era kitchen painted off-white, with linoleum-topped counters, cabinets, a sink, and a giant clock with Roman numerals. I can't remember exactly what Patricia and I fought about sitting at the table between the dishwasher and the fridge decorated with the girls' drawings. Anything and everything, I suppose, the arguments being the icy surface of a deep lake frozen by a growing emotional chasm. Around the corner and past the dining room, Ursula and Isadora would be in the living room half-heartedly drawing with crayons or playing distractedly with their stuffed animals. For they were listening to the sharp voices emerging from the kitchen and tearing at their childhood Eden.

A divorce often dissipates a lot of bad energy, the way a lightning rod bears away an intense atmospheric charge. Still, while this emotional release may be an absolute necessity, many things of beauty are often lost. Once Patricia and I separated, the girls never returned to Escalante Forks. Those waters still flow through ponderosa pines and granite cliffs under the western sunlight, but Ursula and Isadora are no longer a part of that river's flow.

≈≈≈

Here where I stood deep in the Dominquez Canyon, the sun had long since slid below the cliff edge, and the earth's shadow now engulfed the entire gorge. A cold wind suddenly riffled the creek's surface, biting through my flannel shirt and rocking the faultless nest in its willow tree. It was time to go.

Retracing my steps, I followed the trail downstream back to the cacti garden. In the shadows of early evening, it was not the attractive place it had been before. Instead, it was cold, dark, and full of thorns. Therefore, I marched on. I quickly reached the fork in the Little Dominquez trail and crossed the creek. Climbing up out of the creek bed, I headed north towards the Gunnison River.

To my left, the sandstone walls reached for a somber blue zenith. Behind the western cliffs, scattered clouds were brush strokes of red and orange. While there was still enough light to make my way, impenetrable shadows edged the canyon floor, and the gold on the cottonwoods had dulled as if corroded by the passage of decades. My boots crunched on the shattered quartz that lined the empty trail. The canyon had become a lonely place.

When we split up, Patricia left Delta to move to Grand Junction. For a time, I kept the 1920's house with the linoleum counters and the Roman numeral clock. I also had the girls full-time, though every other weekend they would stay with their mother in one of the city's turn-of-the-century houses that had been sub-divided into apartments. In the summer, on a Sunday evening, Patricia's shaded windows would spill yellow light into the warm, soft air, lighting up the street's dusty Siberian elms. I would knock on the door, it would open, and the girls would show me their latest project – glitter covered abstract drawings or plastic masks decorated with pipe cleaner whiskers and Magic Marker rimmed eyes. My estranged wife would stay in the background, tightly smiling, the floor lamp illuminating her dark blond hair, the high cheekbones on her Slavic face creating sharp shadows.

At last, the girls would hug their mother good-bye, and they would follow me back down the stairs to the waiting car. Ursula would calmly get in the back. However, Isadora, seven years old, would sit in the front seat, because as the car pulled into the nighttime streets, moving past living room windows emitting blue television light and under streetlamps glowing like a series of false moons, she would begin to softly weep. And then, about the time we reached the bridge over the Colorado River, its dark waters bisecting the city, the crying would build to wracking sobs and she would bury her head in my lap, her whole body shaking. This would last until we passed through the town of Whitewater, about a dozen miles south of the city. Finally, while we crossed the lightless expanse of shale hills between Grand Junction and Delta, her crying would settle, and she would peer silently out at the distant stars over the Uncompahgre Plateau, where the unseen waters of the Escalante Creek still carved its ancient granite banks.

A year after the separation, I too moved to Grand Junction. I rented a small, two-bedroom house half a block from the university where I teach, and the campus with its straight-lined brick buildings and concrete paths became the girls' playground. The biology building had a courtyard with trees, flowers, benches, a sundial, and a meandering artificial stream with a brass heron perched on one leg. This became their favorite place to act out intricate fantasies on long Saturday afternoons. But the heron never flew into the quadrilateral sky, and they couldn't swim in the metal-lined creek that led nowhere.

At my new house, the front door opened on a fair-sized living room with a beige armchair, a too-white modular couch, and a decades old television set, which stood next to the hall that bisected the rest of the dwelling. The other rooms branched off from this hallway, including the kitchen, which had an indoor rectangular window that faced this inner passage. The girls' bedroom was the next room down, diagonally placed across the hall. They used to sleep with their door open, and thus, at night, when I would sit at the kitchen table reading under its single overhead lamp, I could glance through the window and see them, illuminated by the hall light, tucked into their futon on the floor, their blue eyes closed, their narrow faces relaxed, lips partly opened, blond hair a halo on their pillows. I always felt profoundly comforted in those moments, as if by seeing my daughters through the window's tightly defined frame, I was seeing a true image – an ontological portrait of contentment, harmony, and protection.

But now, as I crossed the darkening canyon and thought back on those change-filled days, I realized that this image had been illusory, a momentary alignment of glass and space. There was no getting around it – the early years of their childhood had been a sheltering Eden, but when the hidden tensions between their parents surfaced, that Eden dissipated. Deep within, Ursula still feels the instability from a decade of living between multiple homes that continually changed, and Isadora still weeps from those long, dark rides returning from her mother's apartment. Meanwhile, their perfect nest abides silent and abandoned in a deep granite gorge, open and empty to the wind and the rain and the dust formed from rock two billion years old.

Entering the bend in the canyon, I started towards the Gunnison River. Passing the wood corral, which looked centuries old in the fading light, I crossed through the wire gate and reached the canoeists' campsite beside the river. Several campfires sent flames and smoke towards the evening sky, as campfires have done on the Uncompahgre Plateau for over ten thousand years.

Wanting to get back to my car before nightfall, I kept up my pace, striding down the trail between the Gunnison and the dimly lit cliffs. I had just reached the bridge when an alien noise swallowed the sounds of flowing waters – the rumble of approaching freight engines. In moments, from around the bend across the river, two canary yellow Union Pacific diesels crawled through the turn, their roaring echoing between the sandstone walls, their horn blasts like angelic trumpets. Behind the engines rolled an eternal line of aluminum coal cars, each loaded with the compressed remains of ancient jungles.

Time. It was time objectified that slid past. As I watched that great metallic reptile slide down the riverine canyon, I considered that we all dwell in Eden until the snake of time enters our lives, bringing with it troubles – a painful fall on a rough stone pathway, a deep cut from a clumsily held knife, a wasp sting, a father's angry words, a friend's betrayal on the playground, a beloved dog's death. As we age, the dark moments pile up, and at some point – we rarely know exactly when – we depart the garden, never to return. And this is how it must be. Unless they are devastatingly destructive, life's challenging experiences – the people and events that seemingly oppose us – are instead the forces that ultimately shape us, molding us into our true selves. As Carl Jung explains, in order to grow and transcend our childhood state of dependency, we must suffer the wounds of the quest, heal, and move on, forever leaving the garden behind us. So I had to place my faith in time and trust that as the years pass, my daughters' Edenic wounds will fade, and they will realize that the divorce was necessary, even desirable – not only for their parents, but for them as well.

Still, as the rear engine of the coal train added its reverberations to the canyon, and its dim headlamp receded down the tracks, I knew I would always be haunted by an image of two girls playing in the laughing waters between granite walls, and an empty warbler's nest fading in the silver light of the Uncompahgre dusk.

A Trick of Light and Shadow

When she knocked on my open office door, I looked up from a student essay I was loading up with red marks.

"Yes?" I asked.

"Professor Nizalowski?" a woman asked in a clear, contralto voice. "I have been told that you are an expert on mythology."

"Well, I wouldn't say I'm an expert. But I do teach classes in it."

Her thin smile paled at that, but she introduced herself anyway and continued on. "I was wondering if you could help me with a matter that concerns the Greek gods."

I was intrigued. It was certainly rare for someone who was not one of my students to come by asking for mythological advice.

"I can try," I said with a nod. "Why don't you take a seat?"

She carefully placed herself in the padded metal frame chair that faces my desk, and her steel blue eyes scanned the rows of books lining the walls. While she did this, I studied her. She wore dark slacks and a loose grey blouse. A black leather satchel hung from her shoulder. Tall and fine-featured, she had an angular, aristocratic face. Her long hair, pulled back in a severe pony-tail, had once been pure black. It now held threads of grey that added a certain dignity to her persona. Her gaze had reached the upper shelves and their mythological texts – *Masks of God* by Joseph Campbell, *Symbols of Transformation* by Carl Jung, *The Goddesses and Gods of Old Europe* by Marija Gimbutas, *From Primitives to Zen* by Mircea Eliade, and so forth. The shadowy smile returned, but when her eyes dropped to meet mine, there was something unnerving about them. She peered at me for perhaps a minute, and then explained her purpose in visiting me.

"About six months ago, my maternal granduncle died in Scotland," she began. "He was a retired army major, and since he had no wife or children, his estate went to his sibling's only child – my mother. The estate wasn't much really, mostly mementos of his years of service. There were several pieces that my mother gave to me, and amongst them was a rather curious metal badge.

"My granduncle was an officer in the Royal Scots, the oldest Scottish regiment in the British Army. As an officer, he had the right to wear a bronze badge emblazoned with the regiment's crest – a kind of sunburst with Christ at the center holding a crosspiece. One day I was studying this badge when I found an engraving so fine I needed a jeweler's glass to make it out. What does that suggest to you?"

"I have no idea," I replied a bit tersely, wondering what all of this had to do with Greek mythology.

She frowned at my obtuseness. "That only a select few are meant to know the engraving is there."

After a pause, I asked, "Why is the image a secret?"

Once again those strange, blue eyes drilled into mine, as if she were deciding if she could trust me. "What do you know about the Knights Templar?"

"Not much past their role in the Crusades."

"Do you know about their violent end?"

I shook my head.

"In 1312, at the request of King Philip of France, Pope Clement the Fifth disbanded the order, and Philip then unleashed a campaign of violence and terror on the Knights Templar. Those who survived fled to Scotland, where the order continued in secret. They would identify each other with a covert image, one that mixed their Christian and pagan roots – the figure of Athena riding a stallion."

"Why Athena?"

"The Knights Templar were, of course, mounted warriors, and it's my understanding that Athena is associated with horses."

"Well, yes, that's true. Though usually the Greek deity most linked with horses is Poseidon. Yet, Athena is said to have invented the chariot, and therefore she was invoked when horses were used in warfare."

"Exactly. So, I believe that this engraving on my granduncle's badge would prove what my mother has always claimed – that her family is descended from the Knights Templar."

All of this struck me as rather fantastic. Still, one never knew. Oddity alone is not a reliable indicator of falsehood.

"So, where do I come in?"

"I'm not absolutely certain if the woman in the engraving is indeed Athena. If she is not, then the engraving may have nothing to do with the Knights Templar. This would cast grave doubt on my mother's story about our ancestry."

"Describe the figure on the horse."

"She is a helmeted woman dressed in flowing robes, bearing a shield and a spear. On the shoulder that faces us, she has a grimacing mask surrounded by a tangle of snakes."

"The Gorgon's head!" I exclaimed. "Perseus gave it to Athena in gratitude for her help in killing Medusa."

A look of triumph flashed across the woman's face. She leaned anxiously forward in her seat. "I have the badge with me. Would you study it, and confirm that the figure is indeed Athena?"

"Of course. I would very much like to see this engraving."

She reached into the black satchel and pulled out a small jeweler's glass and an object wrapped in a clean white cloth. After setting down the jeweler's glass, she carefully unfolded the cloth, revealing the object. It was as she had described it – a bronze oval about two and a half inches high surrounded by a sunburst design. At the center, a figure of Christ held a large "X", and underneath him was an arc bearing the words "The Royal Scots."

"Turn it over and look at the back," she ordered.

To my surprise, the back was solid. I had expected the badge to be hollow, like a carnival trinket. There was a large pin to affix the badge to a wool jacket or khaki shirt.

"Where's the Athena engraving?" I asked, finding no sign of it.

"You need the jeweler's glass to see it," she explained as she picked up the small black cylinder and placed it in my right hand. "Look at the bottom of the arc, about where Christ's feet are resting on other side."

Placing the jeweler's glass to my eye, I did as she directed. In the lens, the badge's smooth back loomed large, like the surface of a planet seen through a telescope. Its bronze metal glinted in the overhead fluorescent lighting. With growing unease, I scanned the badge. All I could see were random scratches. No horse. No shield and spear. No helmeted Athena.

"Well, what do you think?" came the contralto voice from over my left shoulder. "Is it Athena? Do you see the snakes?"

I felt a rising panic. This woman desired a confirmation that her maternal line possessed a deeply rooted connection with the medieval Knights Templar. An entire family myth had probably grown up around this story, a generational tale that she fervently believed. It had become such a fundamental part of her being that she had transformed arbitrary scrapes on a military badge into an elaborate illusion of a Templar talisman. Yet, there was nothing there.

What was I going to say?

~~~

We usually accept that observation and reality have an absolute correspondence, but the actual relationship between seeing and truth is fraught with complex ambiguities. The eyes can be a powerful tool to verify the truth – seeing is believing, after all. However, there are times when surface appearances trick us, and we therefore fail to grasp the deeper reality of what we are viewing. A rabid squirrel looks harmless, but it is actually quite dangerous. Also, we can mistake false images for reality, like the aquatic mirages formed in the deep desert when rising heat waves distort the light. The false lakes created by this distortion look remarkably real, and they have drawn many a traveler desperate for water to their deaths.

However, there are times when hallucinations like these can reveal the truth instead of concealing it, indicating significant verities beneath their illusory veils.

On Colorado's western edge, there is a sizable uplift in the earth's crust called the Uncompahgre Plateau. At its heart, the Dominguez Creek has carved a canyon that stretches over twenty miles from the Dominguez Ridge to the Gunnison River. The canyon is named for Francisco Atanasio Domínguez, who, along with Silvestre Vélez de Escalante, travelled through western Colorado during the two priests' 1776 expedition to find a northern route connecting Santa Fe to the Spanish missions of California.

The mouth of the Dominguez Canyon opens at a point where the Gunnison River bends through almost every point of the compass before returning to its original northwestern flow, all of it through Triassic sandstone cliffs. Here, the Dominguez Canyon leaves the river and splits into two branches. One meanders in a southerly direction, the other veers west, and this latter branch holds the finest wonders – a fifty-foot waterfall that plunges over a two-billion-year-old Precambrian granite ledge, several window rocks cut into rust-colored sandstone spires, and a half-dozen panels of centuries old Ute and Fremont Indian petroglyphs. On these panels, shamans, ghostly figures with square heads and shoulders, stand beside stylized mountain sheep, sun emblazoned shields, and abstract structures of lines and circles. Along both Dominguez Canyon branches, groves of ancient cottonwoods line the streambed.

One midwinter's day, I was hiking in the Dominguez Canyon. The morning had dawned sunny and cloudless, and its clarity had drawn me to the high desert. After a short drive, I left my car and followed a dirt road along the Union Pacific rail line to where a pedestrian bridge spans the Gunnison River. Once over the river, I strode alongside it to the Dominguez Canyon's mouth, where I hiked along a well-worn trail past a concrete irrigation dam, through a wire gate, and along the canyon's ninety-degree bend. Being winter, the cottonwoods were bare, their dark grey branches forming web-works against the blue sky. The stream was flowing strong, and I could hear it whenever the trail veered towards the creek. Ice rimmed its banks. Underfoot, scattered crystals from time-shattered Cambrian quartzite glittered in the sun. Juniper, pinon, saltbush, and sage dotted the slopes flowing out from the beige and red sandstone walls that rose hundreds of feet.

It was already well past noon when I reached the fork and took the western channel towards the petroglyphs and waterfalls. Yet, despite the short winter's day, I journeyed far enough up-canyon to reach the petroglyphs and contemplated the shamanic figures with their wedge-shaped bodies and eyeless, square heads, sometimes topped by stylized horns. Several of the shaman were next to depictions of game animals – deer, mountain sheep, antelope – and were clearly drawing in these creatures to be hunted. There were also concentric circles, mysterious discs, and abstract shapes that brought to mind the cryptic drawings of Paul Klee. Finally, there were images of warriors on horseback, their feathered headdresses prominently displayed. These were clearly Ute figures from after the Spanish arrival.

Departing the petroglyphs, I trekked back down-canyon to the falls and settled in to study their smooth granite channels, sunbaked ledges, and fifty-foot descent. Lost in the language of water, I ignored the day's passage, and when I finally left the falls, the sun had nearly reached the southwestern horizon.

Not wanting to be caught on the Uncompahgre Plateau in the dark, I quickly moved down the trail. I had passed through the fork and reached a stone shelter built by Ute hunters, when I glanced up at the canyon's west wall. There, on its rim, stood a man.

Startled, I stopped and gazed up at this figure several hundred feet above me. Dark and implacable against the silver-blue sky, he had broad, almost square shoulders, a blocky head, and a wide torso. His legs were out of sight behind a low boulder. Despite staring straight at me, he neither waved nor called out.

In those days, there were rumors that an old man lived in a cabin somewhere along the Dominguez Canyon's south branch, and at first I thought the figure on the cliff might be this mythical denizen. But the more I peered at the silent figure, the more it reminded me of the shamanic petroglyphs I had been examining before descending to the falls. Was this a Ute deity, I wondered, manifesting in an elder place of worship? Unnerved by this thought, I broke into a half-run down the trail. Every ten yards or so I would pause and look back over my shoulder. The figure never moved, but it did seem to be following my progress.

When I reached the canyon's bend, where it turned towards the Gunnison River, I stopped and studied the figure. Quite diminutive now, it still had not moved, and once I caught my breath, I began to laugh. The more I examined the figure, the more I became convinced that it was a juniper tree mimicking the shamanic shapes of the ancient petroglyphs. By the time I reached my car in the near darkness, I was absolutely certain that it had been a juniper tree playing tricks and creating an illusion of an ancient spirit. Turning the key, I started the engine and headed for home.

However, some months later, when I returned to the Dominquez Canyon I decided to test my theory. I stood next to the same Ute hunting shelter and studied the cliffs. Nothing. There was a cluster of juniper trees on the ledge, but none of them appeared shamanic. Of course, it wasn't sunset and it was a different time of year, early spring. Perhaps in the changed light, the visual effect was not the same. Or the juniper could have been lost in a cliff slide. Or my mind was not in a sufficiently receptive state.

But then again, on that earlier hike, perhaps I actually did see a shaman or a shamanic deity. If our Euro-American rational view of the universe is incomplete, it may be possible that a Ute Indian shaman who lived centuries ago could traverse time and materialize in our electronic era. Or, conceivably, the shamanic gods themselves are real – square shouldered deities of sun, rain, lightning, and the hunt who dwell in the deep canyons, appearing only at dusk to solitary travelers.

A final possibility is the archetypal explanation. Carl Jung argued that there are objective, psychic structures that dwell in the deep unconscious. These patterns have resulted from our species' interaction with the universe, configurations of consciousness born in the interface of the senses with the physical and energetic world. Jung called these patterns archetypes. When these original forms emerge into the light of our consciousness, they inspire the gods, myths, and legends of every culture across all the vast ages of humanity.

On that first hike, when I saw the shamanic figure on the canyon rim, I had been studying the pre-Columbian Indian petroglyphs, and those images may well have stirred the archetypal patterns in my unconscious, causing them to rise and become manifest in the outer world in the form of a shaman standing on the cliff, peering down at me.

Anthropologists have long observed the archetypal power and significance of the American Indian rock art of the Southwest. Writing about the 3000-year-old Barrier Canyon style pictographs found in the desert labyrinths of eastern Utah, Polly Schaafsma states in *Indian Rock Art of the Southwest*, "Many shamanic practices and much of the symbolism associated with shamanism are held in common over vast areas, and the Barrier Canyon Style anthromorphs have attributes and associations characteristic of shamans throughout the world." Dennis Slifer, in *The Serpent and the Sacred Fire: Fertility Images in Southwest Rock Art*, writes, "The fascinating images of petroglyphs and pictographs span thousands of years of American Indian culture. . . . The recurrent themes of sexuality, death, and regeneration are, in fact, archetypal, occurring in myths and prehistoric images from cultures around the planet."

This is a major source of a petroglyph's power. While American Indian rock art is certainly rooted in the unique cultural and spiritual attributes of the peoples who created them, they also evoke vital archetypes universal to us all, and I believe on that winter day in Dominguez Canyon, its ancient petroglyphs summoned shamanic archetypes from my deep unconscious and projected them on that canyon rim in the form of a 1000-year-old shamanic deity. So, even if it were simply a trick of light and shadow, that vision held a profound truth. Whether it was a deity, an archetype, or a simple illusion, the shamanic figure I witnessed in Dominguez Canyon revealed a profound truth – the fundamental connection between the elder peoples of that canyon, the natural world, and the spirit realm, an intertwining beautifully revealed in the rocks and trees and flowing waters of that strange and wondrous place.

≈≈≈

There have been other moments when illusions, or rather what we name illusions, have revealed to me threads from the underlying weave of reality. However, only one of my encounters with the illusory shattered me so thoroughly that I felt as if I had learned God's dark secret.

This vision took place decades ago, when I was far younger and more daring in my journeys beyond the boundaries of reason and mundane perception.

One frigid November night, I was standing around a campfire with a circle of
friends and strangers midway up a peak on the Sierra Nevadas. The windless
night was perfectly clear, and the stars shone like backlit gems of pure ice. A
quarter moon illuminated the surrounding snow-covered mountains in a ghostly
white light. We were near a set of frozen waterfalls in a grove of cottonwoods,
their branches bereft of leaves. Beyond the trees, the slopes were bare granite and
scrub pine.

We had been standing around this fire for maybe an hour when a plastic
bag started around the circle. The conversation faded, and the night grew silent.
The bag was nearly filled with psilocybin mushrooms. When the bag reached me,
I drew out a broken cap and chewed on it solemnly. The taste was earthy and bitter; the texture like half-melted rubber. Upon completing the circle, the bag went
around again. This time I drew out a partial stem and just a sliver of a cap.

Then we waited.

The fire burned and snapped, its oranges and reds grew richer in color, its
shapes sharper, like yucca leaves turned to flame. The conversation picked up
again, the voices becoming almost shrill. Not knowing many people in the circle,
I remained quiet. Time passed like the ticking of ice on a frozen lake. The drug
began to wash over me, like a rising flood. I had done psilocybin before, and I
had always experienced an embracing euphoria accompanied by pleasant visions.
But these mushrooms were more potent than any I had previously encountered.

As the moon crept towards the jagged western horizon and the midnight
stars reached their zenith, my consciousness shifted with them. At some point,
I slipped past the grey borderline of being too high. I knew it was a frightening
place since I had encountered it once before on L.S.D., and when I realized that I
had again entered that chaotic realm, I panicked. Suddenly, the campfire became
disturbing, its consumption of the wood logs an act of violence. I grew paranoid
of the circle, their dark forms, dressed in heavy coats and wool caps, appeared
ominous, somber, secretive. They kept glancing at me and then murmuring
amongst themselves, as if plotting against me.

Finally, I broke from the circle and stumbled towards the frozen stream,
the snow crunching loudly under my boots. Away from the fire, I felt the clear,
frigid night like a hammer blow. Leaning against a granite boulder, I studied my
surroundings. I became intensely aware of the cottonwood trees, their apparently
dead, bone-white branches etched by moonlight.

These mortality-filled trees repelled me, and so I stepped away from my
boulder and drifted out onto the open slopes. There I had an unobstructed view

of the dome of the sky ablaze with stars. Perseus loomed overhead with Medusa's head in hand, Taurus the Bull was falling upwards, and Orion, the hunter, was slipping out from the world's eastern edge. Gazing at the stars of Orion's belt – Alnilam, Mintaka, Alnitak – I started reciting the poem "Burning the Small Dead," in which Gary Snyder sums up the existence of whitebark pine, Mt. Ritter, and the constellations themselves as "windy fire." All of this is going to end, I thought – the cottonwoods, the Sierra Nevada, Orion's stars, the entire universe – all of it. Nothing will escape. In response to this vision of inexorable and total entropy, the stars shook, the boulders vibrated, the mountainside shimmered, as if the cosmos itself were breaking up. I crouched down and began to weep, my mind flitting between images of my father, grey mustache and hair neatly combed by some anonymous nurse, expiring in a bed of white hospital sheets, and the distant and invisible sun dying beneath my icy feet.

Finally, someone noticed that I had left the campfire and came in search of me. When she asked what was wrong, my inarticulate murmurings about the end of the cosmos led her to gently guide me back to the fire, where several of my friends walked me to the trailhead where we all slid into a car and drove down iron-hard dirt roads barely illuminated by the setting moon. After nearly an hour, we reached a pinewood cabin where I huddled in an armchair under a red wool blanket and wept until dawn, overwhelmed with the knowledge that all things must die. Finally, with the rising of the sun, someone turned off the standing lamp, and I slid into a deep sleep.

When I awoke, I was alone. The room was bathed in a bright golden glow. I got up from the armchair, walked stiffly over to the window, and pulled back the red flannel curtains. The window afforded a fine view of the mountain park that held the cabin, its broad oval covered in snow and outlined by deep stands of ponderosa pine. High in a blue sky, the sun poured forth, bathing the high sierras in a blessed light that made the night's psilocybin phantasmagoria fade like the memory of a moonlit city glimpsed from a passing train.

As I peered out at that snowbound alpine meadow, I realized that my midnight despair at the endgame's total void had emerged from a mind and spirit trapped in linear time. And there is a truth in that vision, for our material selves dwell in the physical universe where, according to the laws of entropy, time runs in a one-directional arrow, and at the arrow's end all life, matter, and energy dissipates. However, our ultimate being dwells above time's arrow, in a realm where time is circular, more like a fathomless lake than a flowing stream. In this dominion of the Pueblo Indians' Sun Father, whom Ralph Waldo Emerson named the

Universal Mind, we exist in a state with no boundaries. We become, in the words of Joseph Campbell, "an intelligible sphere whose center is everywhere and circumference is nowhere." In my life, both before and after this nightmarish experience in the Sierra Nevadas, I have encountered manifestations from this sacred terrain, including the shaman in Dominguez Canyon.

Still, as a fundamental condition of a cosmos formed from matter and energy, linear time is an essential aspect of our existence. It is the apple in the Garden of Eden. To exist in the physical universe, we must eat the apple and embrace linear time, thereby accepting the knowledge that birth leads inexorably to death. That is the truth I confronted in those frightening hallucinations that devoured me on that Sierra Nevada mountainside – the real essence found in the maze of that night's illusions.

≈≈≈

And so, what was I going to say to this woman with her Royal Scots badge?

I glanced up from the metallic object in my hands. She was still peering at me with those piercing blue eyes, pleading, waiting for an answer. Perhaps I just needed to view the badge in the right way. Frowning, I studied it again through the jeweler's glass, turning it under my fluorescent desk lamp. All I could see were the scattered, meaningless scratches.

However, as I admired the flash of reflected light off its shining surface, I realized that there was a deeper truth behind this woman's vision of the badge, a kind of revelatory wisdom that had been handed down generation after generation, and I was not willing to dig out such profound roots and burn them before her, thereby destroying her faith and replacing it with my own.

At last, I set down the jeweler's glass and handed the badge back to her.

"Yes," I said. "It is very difficult to see, but there is a figure of a woman on horseback, facing to the side, spear and shield in hand. And on her shoulder is the Gorgon's head with its bundle of snakes, confirming that she is indeed Athena."

"Thank you!" she exclaimed. "I knew she was there, but I needed someone who had the knowledge to recognize the figure to confirm my observations. You have done wonderfully! I truly appreciate your time."

Once she had placed the badge and the jeweler's glass in her satchel, we stood and she coolly offered her hand, which I gently shook and quickly released. With a departing smile that was a distinct contrast to her cobalt eyes, she left through the still open door.

I sat back down and picked up the piece of petrified wood I keep on my desk. About the size of my palm, it is jet black and polished by the winds of the remote Utah canyon where I found it. Reflecting the light, it reminded me of the woman's Royal Scot's badge, a shaman standing in the dusky light of winter, and a place in the Sierra Nevada where the stars shook. For reasons I didn't fully comprehend, the associations pleased me.

Finally, I set the petrified wood back in its place to the left of my keyboard, and with a smile of my own, got back to work.

Four Meditations on the Death of John Lennon

I

In the late 1960's, my brother would place his stereo's speakers in the upstairs bedroom window and blare *Sergeant Pepper's Lonely Hearts Club Band* across the hazy, upstate New York summer evenings. One night, the last, low resonance of "A Day in the Life" droned along the blue dusk fields. The fireflies filled the night with a flashing green galaxy of sparks. To the south, distant lightning pulsed, vague yellow flares accompanied by low, lazy thunder. Miles to the north, a train blew its moaning, time-passing-around-the-bend whistle.

II

One fall, I hitched to Syracuse, New York, and drifting through college town, I stayed with strangers. My first night, two Syracuse University forestry majors broke into a vacant apartment across the hall from theirs so I could have a place to crash. Using my backpack for a pillow, I slept fitfully, fully dressed, on a brown blanket I'd placed beside the back door. Come morning my eyes snapped open to the sound of the front door opening. The voice of an older woman showing the apartment echoed through the empty rooms. I grabbed my belongings, slammed open the back door, and dashed down the stairs. Running through a cold, narrow alley, I plunged into a sun-filled street, losing myself in the Saturday crowds milling about the boutiques and headshops.

The next night was a lot calmer.

I stayed in the university dorms with a prelaw sophomore. He was blue-eyed and round-faced, and wore short brown hair, a baggy Led Zeppelin t-shirt, and loose khakis. His roommate was gone for the weekend, and while he'd been dreaming of having sex with someone unknown woman, he decided to settle for conversation with a young bearded wanderer instead. After smoking several slender joints, we listened to Lennon's *Imagine* album. The line, "Imagine there's no heaven," kept running through my mind as I slid into a deep sleep on a soft bed, the fear of returning landladies wonderfully absent.

Soon after sunrise, I stood at the mouth of an onramp, thumb out, heading south on Interstate 81.

III

In Newark, Delaware, I had a friend, a scholar of Romantic poetry, who owned all of John Lennon's albums. We'd spend evenings drinking bourbon while discussing Islamic architecture, Alan Watts, Goethe's *Theory of Color,* the music of King Crimson, and L.S.D. Often Lennon played on the stereo, an anarchist backdrop to our post-60's intellectual excursions.

Several months earlier, my father had died of a heart attack, and when I would picture him hooked into the beeping machines, tubes down his throat, morphine drip preventing his speech, the lines to "Instant Karma" possessed a meaning that's lost on me now.

Typically, around 3:00 a.m. I'd leave my friend's place and head for my apartment, walking with uncertain steps along the quiet, sycamore lined streets. After several blocks I'd leave the street for a dirt path that cut through a dense cluster of staghorn sumac, crossed two sets of B&O Railroad tracks, and entered a century-old cemetery. If there was a full moon, the tracks would glint with a silvery light. Sometimes, when I was feeling particularly low, I'd sit on the rails, chant the words from "Instant Karma," and wait for a train.

That train never came for me, but years later, in a different form, it came for my friend.

IV

On the day John Lennon died, I wore a black armband to class. My university students didn't understand. I babbled the entire period about conspiracy theories and Ronald Reagan's war on the counterculture.

Back home, the radio played Beatles songs all day. When my fiancé arrived from work, she asked me to turn it off. When I protested that Lennon had been shot, she said she knew, but that she had really heard enough Beatles for one day.

So, I turned off the radio.

And that's when the thread of memories became mist, the mist transmuted into tears, and the tears tracked across my face, tears of magic and loss, creation and destruction, drum and flame – a Shiva dance of time.

THE EPHEMERAL HOURS

I was driving through White Mesa, a small town in the western reaches of the Ute Mountain Reservation, when I saw the apparition.

It was late afternoon in mid-March. High above, a pale sun shone through sheer clouds. Around me, the scattering of simple, rectangular government houses bled out onto a broad plateau sparsely covered in dark green junipers. A line of power poles, each with a single crosspiece, receded into the vast spaces ahead where Utah's Abajo Mountains rose in blue, layered mounds. Behind me, visible in the rear-view mirror, stood Ute Mountain, its rounded volcanic peaks forming the shape of a man asleep, his arms crossed over his chest. According to Ute mythology, one day the sleeping giant that is Ute Mountain will rise up and walk the land, signaling the end of the world.

As I approached the town's northern edge, a kind of vision appeared ahead and to my right, so I slowed down. A thin old man in jeans and a blue denim shirt sat cross-legged just past the highway's shoulder. His face was narrow and bony, with stark black brows and loose grey hair tucked under a red bandana. When I drew near him, he aimed his blazing gaze right at me and began making strange motions with his hands and arms, the glyph of an Egyptian dancer come to life. His gestures were rapid, unnerving, magical. I watched him in the mirror after I passed, and I could see that he kept performing his divinatory gestures until he disappeared around a curve in the highway.

Whether the Ute elder was blessing me, cursing me, or performing a ceremony that had nothing to do with me, I will never know. It was one of those brief encounters that reveal the underlying mystery of existence. In these moments the world unfolds, dropping its masks, uncovering dualistic archetypes from the deep unconscious, an alchemical surprise that shapes our understanding of the world as a place of random delight or terror, discovery or loss.

The ephemeral hours.

≈≈≈

Just a few miles south of Galisteo, a small village in northern New Mexico, there stands an igneous dike, a ridge of stone thrusting up out of the earth like a high wall of granite. This one, named Comanche Gap, starts at the slopes of the Ortiz Mountains and runs far out into the eastern plains of the Galisteo Basin. Covered in petroglyphs carved by the Pueblo Indians of the 14th and 15th centuries, the stone faces of Comanche Gap hold images of stars, butterflies, horned serpents, masks, and shields. It was a place of war, where many pitched battles were fought between the settled, agricultural Pueblos and the migratory marauders from the prairies. Therefore, the carved images celebrate the war gods, evoking a fierce and compelling mysticism. It was one of my favorite places to explore when I lived in Santa Fe.

One windy March day, under high clouds and a polarized sun, I climbed up to Comanche Gap from the nearby highway. The wind was so strong that I had to battle my way to the stone heights. I tried to study the petroglyphs, but my eyes watered in the stiff breeze. Seeking shelter, I found a shallow depression in the rocks. Its stone walls cut the wind significantly, and I was finally able to look around me without shielding my eyes and ducking my head. Above, a massive shield graced the stone face, its circular surface decorated with sun and star symbols. Two ferocious faces, grimacing and barring their teeth, peered out from its center. It seemed to me that this shield was protecting me from the powerful winds.

Standing beneath the shield, I peered out across the Galisteo Basin, a vast rolling expanse covered with dry grasses and the occasional juniper tree. The wind had lifted whole clouds of dust into the air, a veritable desert elevated into the sky. The late afternoon sun, hovering just above the Ortiz peaks, painted the whole scene a pale yellow, so that the very air shimmered. I realized that this effect was why the Acoma Indians named March, "the month when the air glows." One could feel the power in the wind, the plains, the stones with the sacred markings, and the dike itself, all illuminated by the shining air.

I stayed past sunset, sitting there under the stone shield. As the sky darkened, the wind gradually died down, becoming a mere whisper. Finally, I climbed down the stone dike as an evening quiet settled into the basin, and the first stars appeared in the east.

≈≈≈

On Holy Thursday, a vigil takes place in Catholic churches from the end of evening mass until dawn, a night watch held for the revealed communion host. When I was in my early teens, I used to join my father in this vigil, usually for a couple of hours near midnight.

The church would be wonderfully silent during that time, a holy place of magic and mysticism. The only electric light was a soft, yellow glass encased bulb over the entrance door. In front, the altar held six lit candles that flickered in the cool air. To the right, at a side altar, the monstrance stood between two candles, its bronze sunburst holding the circular host at its center. Beneath it, a large candle enclosed in red glass signaled the presence of the body of Christ. Other than these lights, the church was dark.

From around the church emerged quiet sounds of others participating in the vigil, mostly men. Some murmured in prayer. Now and then one of the men would shift from sitting to kneeling, and there would be the creaking of the wood kneelers. Occasionally, someone would leave or enter the church, accompanied by footsteps clicking on the maple floor, or the soft boom of a closing door.

As the slow minutes passed, I would gradually cease praying and instead contemplate Jesus in the Garden of Gethsemane, left alone to agonize over the coming crucifixion because his apostles have fallen asleep. After a still greater time, I would stop thinking altogether, and simply gaze at the red candle, a momentary glimpse of the eternal.

≈≈≈

When my daughter Ursula was little, she suffered from the croup. Deep, rattling coughs would shake her petite, four-year old body, giving her no respite. In order for her to sleep, she had to stay upright so her throat and bronchial passages could stay clear. To keep her this way, I would sit through the night in a great red armchair we had placed in one corner of the kitchen, holding her against me, her chest to mine, her head propped on my shoulder until dawn's grey light seeped through the windows. As we rested there, a great steel pot of water mixed with eucalyptus oil boiled on the nearby gas stove. The white-walled kitchen would fill with aromatic steam, like a grove of scented trees after a warm rain. A solitary light, a short fluorescent tube over the sink, cast a pale glow through the steam, forming shadows with wavering lines. I used to place a disc of American Indian flute music on the CD player, set the volume low, and leave it on repeat, so that as the evening hours passed, I would awaken every hour or so to a strange white world bathed in electric moonlight, smelling of rain forest, and floating on the resonances of a cedar instrument.

At these moments, I would place Ursula carefully on the armchair still upright, and fill the pot with more water and oil. Then I would return her to my chest and shoulder and rejoin her in sleep, my arms wrapping her small form against me, the life-giving steam pouring into the air and settling into her lungs, helping her to breathe.

≈≈≈

I held my son's tiny, absolutely still body, enclosed in white cloth, a stocking cap on his head. At first I had refused, but at the last moment the need to connect with him overcame my reluctance. His face was perfect – nose, ears, forehead, chin, closed eyes. His body had been wrapped like a mummy's, so I could not see his hands or feet. The lights in the birthing room were white, but subdued. There were only a few pieces of furniture – a chair, a small table, a nightstand. The nurse-midwife stood off to the side, wearing a rust-red dress. My wife was on the bed, sleeping.

I rocked him gently. I don't know why. There was, of course, no sound of breathing, no crying.

≈≈≈

Trinity Site, the place where the physicists and technicians of the Manhattan Project detonated the first atomic bomb, is a remote place southeast of Albuquerque, New Mexico, out on the grassy reaches of a valley called Jornada del Muerto, the Journey of the Dead. Many historians believe the name derived from the Apache raids on Spanish settlers making their slow way up from El Paso. However, Paul Horgan, author of *Great River*, claims the name was inspired by the death of a Spanish alchemist, who fled the Inquisition with his Pueblo Indian companion to perish mysteriously on that long, north-south valley with its broad basin and shallow ridges.

To reach ground zero, one passes through a gate in a wire-mesh fence adorned with yellow "Caution: Radioactive Materials" signs, and heads up a hard-packed dirt road to an obelisk made from dark, roughly finished volcanic stone. As one walks towards the obelisk, which rests at the bottom of a shallow, grass-covered crater, the crater's horizon gradually rises, an unnerving sensation. A bronze plaque on the front of the obelisk reads: "Trinity Site – Where the World's First Nuclear Device Was Exploded on July 16, 1945."

As described in an earlier narrative, the first time I visited Trinity Site, I stood for a time at the obelisk, studying the plaque. Then I turned and watched the tourists milling about with their cameras. Most of them seemed listless, bored. I set off towards the perimeter fence away from the dirt track between the gate and the obelisk. Out there in the grass, away from any trails, I searched the sandy ground. Maybe ten minutes later my quest was fulfilled. Between two clumps of bunch grass rested a dusty green-grey piece of glass. Trinitite.

Despite the warnings posted at Trinity Site, I picked up the glass lump and held it in my palm. It glinted dully in the blazing sun and was warm to the touch, its smooth surface pitted and cratered. I thought about the morning of July 16th, 1945, when an impossible light brighter and hotter than the sun fused the sand into a sheet of green glass, a part of which I now balanced on my hand. Images of Hiroshima flashed through my mind – skulls seared white in atomic fire lying on dirty brick rubble, twisted girders bent by a giant's hand, shadow burns on a school wall. I slipped the glass shard underneath the grass and sand, and I walked away.

～～～

The Union Pacific train line, after it passes through Moffat Tunnel and crosses the Continental Divide, descends into Denver along the face of the Rocky Mountains, heading through thirty secondary tunnels. The train moves slowly, ponderously, along tracks laid at the edge of steep cliffs affording far off vistas of steely grey mountain flanks, ponderosa pines, aspen forests, and an occasional log house. At the bottom, a boulder filled stream, a concrete dam, a broad reservoir, and a mine with ramps, pulleys, and corrugated metal sheds pass in succession. The passengers view this unfolding panorama through large glass windows, the scene vanishing into each tunnel's black corridor to burst forth again when the tunnel ends, like a slowly flickering movie or like falling asleep and waking to a new day, for with each tunnel the landscape changes – a previously obscured rock escarpment, a different stretch of river, a white-capped summit finally revealed, the sudden blue of a man-made lake – an analogy to the dark and light cycle of rebirth we experience each night.

On a recent train journey, as this sequence of images unfolded, I was

thinking of the passage of days. The train, heading through a series of tight
curves, creaked and groaned like a ship shifting with the tides, and the steel
wheels sang on the welded rails with a high, eerie tone. At last, we emerged from
the high canyons and began our slow glide down the side of the final mountain,
the eastern wall of the Rockies. The Colorado prairie stretched forth below us in
hazy distances all the way to Nebraska and beyond.

Out there was my destination. Summoned by the sale of the family farm,
I was on a journey to my childhood home in upstate New York. While I had
not grown up on the farm, its sale was nonetheless a great loss to me. Purchased
in 1920, the farm over the long decades had passed from my grandfather to my
uncle and finally to my cousin, who, as his health declined, found it impossible
to keep up with the property taxes. And thus, this 250-acre farm which had been
in my family for nearly a century would land in the hands of a stranger from
Pennsylvania whose name was unknown to me.

Staring out the glass at the rolling grasslands, I thought of all that was
slipping away. Childhood memories of wandering the farm's forests of oak, ash,
maple, and white pine. The warm manure smell in the barn, the steady rhythm
of the milking machines, and the cats darting amidst the peacefully eating cows.
Or sitting at the white enamel table in the warm nighttime kitchen with my
grandfather, father, and uncle, listening to them converse in Polish while I sipped
hot, sweet tea and the winter wind howled outside. When I was older, I spent
summers working the broad hay fields under a hot sun – the deep thrum of the
tractor engine, the bales heavy in my hands, the binding twine cutting into my
gloved fingers. On those days the ice water my uncle kept in the tractor's big red
plastic jug was a blessing, though better still were the beers shared at the day's
end, after the sun had set behind the tree covered hills.

On the train, time moved forward, and the mountains fell behind me. As I
peered through the window, the world was inevitably changing. Drifting through
a curve, the train turned into the sun, its light flaring across the tinted glass.
Suddenly, a green glow enveloped the view and was quickly gone. Something
about the color pulled at a memory, but try as I might, I couldn't bring it to
consciousness. And yet, mysteriously, that green flash produced in me deep, tragic
sense of a world lost to history's violence.

≈≈≈

In the final years of my first marriage, I lived with my wife of those days and our
two daughters in a century old house in Delta, a small Colorado ranching town.

Our home was on Delta's outskirts, and just a few blocks away, the rangelands began, leading up to the faint, far-off ridge of the Uncompahgre Plateau, the great flat rise of earth that forms a hundred mile stretch of the state's western border with Utah.

Just south of those same blocks there is town park with a 60-acre lake at its heart. This was where every Fourth of July, Delta would launch its fireworks, affording us a perfect view of this annual display from our back yard. However, when Ursula, my oldest daughter, was a young child, she found the fireworks' sharp cracks and massive booms too frightening to bear. So, every Fourth of July, when the sky grew dark, I would take her by the hand and we would walk upstairs to the attic. There, we would watch the fireworks from the west facing window.

Like most attics, ours was filled with stuff – a few wooden chairs with cracked legs, two unneeded kitchen tables, a stack of rolled posters, and plenty of boxes containing old clothes, receipts, bank statements, letters, photographs, books, vinyl albums, and the like. Midway, a cinderblock chimney rose from the floor and vanished into the ceiling. At the far end, where the window faced the east, I had a desk, a few bookshelves, a space heater for the winter, and a portable swamp cooler for the summer. But at the west end there was nothing but life's detritus. So, for the fireworks viewing, I would grab an old stuffed chair cushion, sit myself down, and place Ursula on my lap. From our floor seat, we would stare out the fly-specked, dusty window. In order to see the fireworks better, we left the light off, so the only illumination came up the stairwell from kitchen below. A bit spookily, the broken chairs and stacked boxes loomed around us in the hot, attic darkness.

At last, a white flash would throw shadows on the boxes behind us. Towards the right, through the window, the fireworks with their fountains of light had begun – the sparkling arcs of light totally silent, the thunders muffled. Ursula, freed from frightful sounds, delighted in the display beyond the glass, cheering for each incendiary umbrella. In the light of the nearby streetlamps, I could see Isadora, Ursula's sister, by the apricot tree below, almost dancing in her joy at the colorful detonations. Her mom stood nearby, pointing out the wonders in the sky.

When the penultimate, frenzied cluster of fireworks faded from the sky, we would sit for a moment to make sure it was truly finished. Then we would stand, brush the attic dust off our clothes, and head downstairs into the bright fluorescent lights of the kitchen. There, Isadora and her mom would join us from outside, and we would finish the night's celebration with chocolate cake and ice cream.

Of course, as Ursula grew older, the day came when fireworks no longer scared her, and she would stand outside in the back yard to view them with everyone else. So, though we didn't realize it at the time, there was one evening when we watched the fireworks from behind the upstairs west window for the last time, and made the final Independence Day descent through the narrow tunnel of the walled attic stairway into the light below.

~~~

I stood at the top of the stairs on the second floor of my grandfather's farmhouse. What once served as an upstairs living room-hallway was now filled with the debris of moving – a cluster of standing lamps by the single window, a stack of particle board rectangles, a black iron teapot resting on a small wooden table, a stack of dusty hardcover books topped by a yellow plastic basket, and an open roll-top desk with an empty green wine bottle, a beige scarf, and a stack of DVD's. The illumination from the window was nearly white – sunlight filtered through a high layer of thin clouds. It gave the pale-walled, oblong room a kind of sheen, like a metallic object in the sky receding into a bank of blazing clouds. Around the room a set of doors of differing sizes lead to bedrooms, a bathroom, an attic – doorways into a vanished past, its scattered light long ago absorbed by the plaster walls, the oak doorframes, the warped, antique glass.

I stood for a time, watched the silent dust motes float in the room's slow currents of air, and remembered how when I would stay overnight on the farm, I would sit in that room and read Zane Grey westerns, take a bath in the old porcelain tub, and then sleep in the narrow bed in the far bedroom.

But when the sunlight dimmed, obscured by a dark cloud, the motes disappeared. So I turned and went down the stairs to the first floor's emptiness. From there, I left the house, never to return.

~~~

It was the afternoon of the annular eclipse.

In an annular eclipse, the moon completely covers the sun, but since the moon is at the farthest arc of its orbit, it leaves a ring of blazing light completely around the dark, lunar disk.

In front of our home in the western Colorado city of Grand Junction, we watched the eclipse through my 4 ¼ inch reflecting telescope. The solar filter made the sun look like a lime colored orb.

The eclipse began humbly – a single small bite of darkness from the sun's circle. We watched in the telescope as the black arc grew larger and larger, covering more and more of the sun, one by one devouring the sunspots that mar the sun's purity with minute spots of grey and black. As the air darkened, the birds started their quiet dusk songs, as if the night had prematurely conquered the day. A strange feeling stirred my stomach, as if I were teetering on a cliff edge. My daughter Isadora, a young woman who would soon leave for college, pointed out the shadows projected through the Siberian elm trees onto the nearby cars, the sidewalk, and the driveway. They were all crescent shaped, echoing the eclipse. She called them a collection of Cheshire cat smiles. Her older sister, Ursula, was busy at the telescope, adjusting the lens. My wife Brenda stood closer to the house where she could stare at the eclipsed sun through the trees, her expression troubled. All three – slender, blond, and eerily lit – seemed like figures from a surrealist painting under that strange, occluded star.

At last the eclipse reached totality, and the shimmering ring was complete.

It was an emblem of universal dualities – light and darkness, science and magic, rationality and intuition, materiality and spirit. But it lasted mere minutes, granting a brief understanding, a momentary explanation. Then the moon shifted, and the emblem vanished.

≈≈≈

Recently, I was hiking in a remote corner of Utah's desert lands called Barrier Canyon. It is a sinuous, red and beige sandstone canyon, reaching nearly a thousand feet from its base to its cliff edge. It is a place of powerful sacredness, holding mummy shaped shamanic pictographs that are five thousand years old and would not look out of place in an Egyptian tomb. Because there are horned snake pictographs in Barrier Canyon, some archeologists believe that it is the birthplace of the cult of Quetzalcoatl, the Plumed Serpent, Meso-American god of dualism – his snake aspect representing the dark earth, his wings the sky and all its light. Perhaps thousands of years ago tribal priests held ceremonies in Barrier Canyon that used the same motions of the arms and torso I witnessed performed by an old Ute Indian at the side of a Utah highway.

I had completed my journey to the pictograph panel called the Great Gallery – with its dark brown depictions of shaman, ghost-shaped gods, and game animals in procession – and was about to make my ascent on the trail that leads up the canyon wall and out. There, at the cliff base, was a stand of Indian rice grass growing out of a sand dune. A stiff wind was blowing up the canyon from the distant Green River, and it was bending the grass so it would make marks in the sand, flowing lines that looked like writing. I stood and watched for perhaps twenty minutes, fascinated by the plant drawing lines of text in the sand, and then erasing them, and then drawing more – all of it in a mysterious language that could only be read by the ancient round-eyed gods of Barrier Canyon's pictographs. And yet, somehow, I sensed it was a language that captured the deliquescence of life, the ritual of death, and the sorcery of rebirth.

Finally, a raven called overhead, its wings whispering harshly in the desert currents. Turning from the writing, I looked up but he flew into the sun, keeping his secrets.

The ephemeral hours.

PART TWO

Only the Sun

"Only the sun goes from light to light; for him there is only the day,
and night is that which is always far from him.
But who shall say at night there is no sun?"
– Antonin Artaud, *The Peyote Dance*

Abraxas

I

It was the summer that Mars and Saturn played with Antares, a strange Scorpio summer. According to astrologers, this configuration of planets with the scorpion's blood-red star signifies dangerous and transitional times. And indeed, I sensed change all around me, far reaching metamorphoses passing from darkness to light to darkness again – the great planetary cycle, the earth tilting back and forth as we make our 584-million-mile voyage around the sun.

Over the years, as we travel this planetary circle, the universe resists our actions, carving the shape of our being. When we grow older, this resistance grows stronger, yet the cycles move more quickly.

That's how it was the summer after I turned 60. Transformations surrounded me, and I observed their inevitable shifting from to shadow to light to shadow again – the moon ascending in the sunset sky to set in the next day's early morning darkness.

II

Mars was in retrograde when I met the raven.

I was staying with my wife Brenda in an historic motor court on the south end of Taos, New Mexico. Built from adobe and stucco, the room blocks formed a large courtyard with long portals and darkly polished vigas. Awkward wooden furniture filled the rooms and prints of crimson vistas hung on the beige walls.

It was late evening. I had just spent several hours reading in one of the rather stiff chairs, and I felt the need to stretch and get a bit of fresh air. Stepping out of our room, I found the courtyard illuminated by only a scattering of electric lamps on short black poles and a handful of 40-watt bulbs suspended from the portal's ceiling. Somber cedar and ewe trees, like hulking bears, absorbed most of the light, leaving the courtyard shrouded in darkness. Undeterred, I entered the gloomy space. Overhead, the sky was cloudy and absolutely black, the air cool and damp from recent rains. Walking to the center, I was studying the forking paths of cedar branches silhouetted against the dim light, when, to my right, a piece of shadow left the roof and landed on a viga's severed end.

It was a raven.

I crept up to within a dozen feet of the midnight bird and peered at it. Its pure black feathers possessed no hint of the purple sheen you see on magpies, and its long, dusty wedge of a beak, killer of infant birds and beasts, was nearly as dark as its feathers. Its eyes, almost invisible in the artificial dusk, stared straight at me. After a few heartbeats, it made that unnerving raven call, like the liquid cough of a dying man, warning me to come no closer. Matching the rhythm of my slow breathing, the raven hopped from viga to viga, its wings barely opening with each jump.

We regarded each other warily for some time, until I decided to edge closer. As I did so, the raven stretched its great black wings, looming massive and intimidating in the uncertain illumination – a figure of death and an ill omen. Just as I got near enough to make out the texture of its feathers, it glared at me and floated up into a deep, hidden crevice in the portal's roof. Like some tricky stage magician, the raven had vanished utterly, leaving me profoundly disquieted. I waited perhaps fifteen minutes for it to reappear, but the misty rain started up again, driving me back inside to the realm of light and warmth.

~~~

After the night's rain, the high desert morning broke clear and bright, banishing the unnerving memory of the raven, or so I thought.

Checking out from the motor court, Brenda and I went to a coffeehouse for breakfast, and then left its warren of wood-framed rooms to wander the town. We started with the plaza, dipping in and out of the souvenir shops with their carved Catholic saints and colorful animal effigies from Mexico. Next, we launched into the Taos maze of diminutive streets, searching the dusty bookstores for rare volumes, or studying the landscape paintings in the gallery windows.

After several hours of drifting through the adobe-lined lanes and cotton-wood shaded courtyards, it was time for us to head south to Santa Fe. But we decided to have lunch first, so returning to the plaza, we entered a basement wine bar built like a stone grotto. Coming in from the bright sunlight, it was like entering a deep catacomb, and we could just make out a set of tall tables with high stools arranged around a backlit oaken bar. We settled on a table by the far stone wall, and a dark-haired woman wearing a white blouse and black slacks came out from behind the bar and brought us menus. Once my eyes adjusted to the lighting, I studied the menu until something made me look up. There, on the wall, not six feet away, hung a pen and ink drawing of a raven.

Disconcerted, I found the banished memory of the previous night's raven returning. Here in this cave drawing were manifested the same ruff of space-dark feathers, the same unflinching obsidian eyes, even the same murderous beak, as curved and sharp as some cruel weapon. Like its living counterpart, the raven portrait mesmerized me, especially its eyes, inspiring troubling memories of my deceased father and son. A cold rain filled my soul.

"So have you decided?"

The pleasant contralto voice, speaking from somewhere above me, pulled my gaze away from the drawing. I peered up at the dark-haired woman for several beats, not comprehending who she was and why she stood there. The raven had eclipsed the workings of my mind like a dark moon covering the sun.

"Sir, are you ready to order?"

A measured degree of impatience had entered her voice.

"Oh, yes, of course," I answered as if dragged from a dream. I glanced down at the menu in desperation and ordered the first red wine that struck my gaze. "I suppose I'll have the Malbec."

Brenda ordered the same, and added a cheese plate, green olives, and sourdough bread, for I had completely forgotten that we were supposed to be eating lunch. The server scribbled on

her pad of paper and then disappeared. I went back to staring at the raven, adding very little to my wife's attempts at conversation, even after the meal arrived.

≈≈≈

Upon finishing the bread and wine, we left the grotto, got in our car, and headed south towards Santa Fe. Brenda was driving, leaving me free to study the land. A heavy ceiling of clouds had rolled in, devouring the morning's clarity and leaving the day grey and occluded. We passed through the cluster of adobe structures and dark green cottonwoods that is Ranchos de Taos, and then darted off across the high sage prairie, the Sangre de Cristo Mountains to our left. After a glimpse of the rocky depths of the Rio Grande Gorge, we began to wind down through volcanic bluffs, finally reaching the village of Pilar, with its tile-roofed homes and narrow orchards. Here, the highway meets the river, which emerges from that great gorge like a vast, roiling snake.

Upon leaving Pilar, the highway meanders southwest through a steep-walled canyon, following the Rio Grande through cliffs of basaltic rock and through the towns of Rinconada and Embudo, where it started to rain, draping the scene in a silver mist. After Embudo, Brenda negotiated a long, deep curve that veered left, and the canyon opened out, revealing extensive vineyards.

And that's where we spotted it.

The body of a mule deer, with a good dozen ravens hopping and flapping on and about the carcass, feasting. The sight startled me, bringing back an experience from ten years past.

One autumn afternoon, I was descending the Uncompahgre Plateau, a forested highland one hundred miles long and twenty-five miles wide on the western border of Colorado. I was heading towards Delta, a ranch town just past plateau's eastern edge, and I had just completed the switchbacks that wind down from the summit's forests of ponderosa pine, mountain hemlock, and white fir, and onto the canyon-carved lower shelf of juniper, sagebrush, and yellow-topped snake-weed. I drove over this prairieland for some time, mostly along the tops of rock benches, catching glimpses of the salmon-colored walls of Cottonwood Canyon to the left and the distant grey peaks of the West Elk Mountains dead ahead. Behind, the pick-up trailed a tall plume of pale dust.

At last, I approached the Narrows. Here, the Cottonwood and Roubideau canyons slice towards each other, leaving a narrow isthmus of land so slender that you can glance down into both canyons from your vehicle. About a half mile before the Narrows, the road makes a sharp S-curve that cuts down into the earth and rock. Emerging from this curve, I once again had an unobstructed view of the plateau's broad plain, where I saw a mysterious and confusing sight.

About fifty yards ahead and to the left, there loomed a dark mounded mass, about the size of a large boulder, but heaving and shifting, like a heap of living rags rising and falling around some dense, hidden core.

Then, as the rattling, shaking truck approached, the enigmatic mass's outer layer exploded into a hundred winged scavengers – vultures, golden eagles, red-tailed hawks, Swainson's hawks, Harris hawks, magpies, and, yes, ravens. The mound beneath this riot of winged flesh-eaters was a dead Hereford cow, rotting in the sun.

While I drove past, the gang of raptors and ravens, startled from their feast, circled just above the corpse. But as the Hereford receded in my rearview mirror, I watched as the great cloud of birds resettled to feed again, just as these ravens a decade later were devouring the mule deer in the Rio Grande Gorge, completing the circle begun by the raven in the portal and continued by the raven in the wine cave – the trickster bird, manifestation of death and despair.

III

We had traveled some distance to see him, a dear friend who had been an older colleague at the university where my wife Brenda and I teach. And while our fields are different – he is a historian and I am a writing professor – we share an admiration for the Transcendentalists, especially the core trinity of Whitman, Emerson, and Thoreau. But what truly connects us is our passion for amateur astronomy.

About five years into my teaching appointment, in the mid-1990's, my friend left western Colorado to become a full professor at a different institution elsewhere in the Intermountain West. However, about two decades into his tenure there, unable to adapt to the increasing use of computerized accountability systems in higher education, and succumbing to a growing irascibility towards students and administrators alike, my friend was pressured into retiring sooner than he wished. This "abrupt dismissal," as he characterized it, had shattered his self-image. Being a professor of 19th century American history was his deepest and most fundamental identity. Even working on his lifelong book-length study on Emerson's role in the abolitionist movement failed to compensate for being at the front of a classroom. He was a lost man.

So there we were, behind his 1920's era white-clapboard home in the shade of a linear jungle of overgrown Siberian elms, enjoying their cool relief from the blazing sun. Our wives had gone inside to get out of the heat, but my friend held me back by the arm, murmuring, "Stay out here for a moment. There's something I want to show you."

Recently, my friend had a benign tumor removed from his kidneys, and he still seemed disoriented, as if the anesthetic had not entirely worn off. Draped in baggy khaki pants and a sage-colored button-down shirt, his tall, bamboo body was uncharacteristically hunched, his gaze plaintive. A purebred German shepherd stood beside him, brown and black head tilted up, waiting to be petted. My friend completely ignored him.

While I waited, he stared for some time at a granite boulder on the house's xeriscaped border, and then he gruffly ordered me to follow him across the spacious yard to a pair of aging sheds in the corner of the property, their unpainted wood sides weathered and cracking. Overhead, a raven circled in the thermals. Several mourning doves landed in the elm branches above the sheds, their voices soft and chattering. In the distance, a radio played a Roy Orbison tune.

My friend approached the nearer shed and began fiddling with the door's steel clasp. It had no padlock; instead, a stick stripped of its bark held it closed. After managing to pull the stick through the clasp's steel loops, he pulled several times at the wood plank door, which had clearly swelled in the heat and gotten stuck on its frame. I was about to offer my help when he gave the door a sharp yank, and it abruptly opened, scraping along the ground as it did so.

Inside it was gloomy and hot, with the dry Egyptian smell of old wood. Sunlight slipped in through the spaces between the walls' vertical boards, creating glowing sheets in the dust motes suspended in the dark air. A cluster of garden tools – shovel, hoe, leaf-rake, and a three-pronged cultivator that looked like a hawk's claw – rested in the far corner. Next to the tools, scattered along the far wall, were a half-dozen wood crates, their once-bright illustrations of peaches and apples faded like old photographs.

And in the shed's center, resting on its tripod, stood my friend's telescope.

It is a six-inch reflector, meaning its primary mirror is six inches in diameter. This parabolic mirror rests at the base of a three-foot long tube, which is open at one end so light from stellar objects can enter, reflect off the main mirror, and hit a smaller mirror suspended within the tube towards its entrance. This mirror directs the light to an eyepiece on the side. A bronze-colored tripod, a set of dense counterweights, two steel support bands, and a diminutive spotter scope complete the instrument.

"I'm thinking of moving back to Maine soon," my friend said, breaking the silence. His voice was raspy, as if he were suffering from allergies, or had picked up smoking again.

"Back home by the sea?" I asked.

"Yeah. Well, anyway, I don't want to ship the scope back east, so I thought you could pack it in your Subaru and take it to Colorado with you."

I was confused. This was his beloved instrument, his window on the planets and stars. He had owned it for as long as I had known him, and I couldn't believe he wanted to part with it.

"Surely, you'll want it Maine," I said. "Why don't I store it for you until you can make arrangements to get it back East?"

"No," he said firmly, with an edge of anger I didn't understand. "I no longer need it. I'm giving it to you."

Shaking my head in disbelief, I considered the situation.

"Tell you what. When you're definitely moving to Maine, give me a call, and I'll come out and pick it up then. Meanwhile, you can keep using it."

He shrugged. "I put the scope in here two, three years ago, and it hasn't been out since."

I looked back at the instrument, its bronze and steel elements glinting in the shed's uncertain illumination. My friend had spent hundreds of hours at this telescope's eyepiece while the light from deep space descended its dark cylinder, sailed through its system of mirrors and lenses, and revealed its beauty. Observing the night skies had been one of his essential passions, but that passion had died under the stress of his radically changed life. And now, this finely wrought device dwelled in a dark space built of wood and nails, cut off from the light of heaven.

IV

Abraxas is the god of duality.

Abraxas is the deity who encompasses both light and dark, male and female, sky and earth, the eagle and the snake, the angel and the demon – the one eternally changing into the other.

In the Greek alphabet, in which each letter also stands for a number, the letters in the name of Abraxas add up to 365. Thus, Abraxas, conceived in the Gnostic and Hermetic traditions, encompasses the earth's voyage around the sun, and with it all the cosmic cycles of time. Abraxas is a great and terrible god, who nurtures and destroys, illuminates and conceals.

I first encountered Abraxas in Hermann Hesse's novel *Demian*. The protagonist, Emil Sinclair, is on a journey of self-discovery as he transitions from adolescence into young adulthood, perhaps the most fraught of human metamorphoses. Sinclair learns about Abraxas from many sources, including his mysterious childhood friend, Max Demian, and Pistorius, a failed priest. However, his most powerful revelations concerning Abraxas come directly through meditation and waking fantasies. At one point, Sinclair paints a portrait of this dual-natured deity:

> The painted face in the lamplight changed with each exhortation – became light and luminous, dark and brooding, closed pale eyelids over dead eyes, opened them again and flashed lightning glances. It was woman, man, girl, a little child, an animal, it dissolved into a tiny patch of color, grew large and distinct again. Finally, following a strong impulse, I closed my eyes and now saw the picture within me, stronger and mightier than before.

Carl Jung, the founder of archetypal theory, took a voyage similar to Sinclair's when he was approaching his thirtieth year in 1914. His was a purposeful descent into the unconscious, a perilous journey with shamanic structure and meaning. It nearly drove him insane. Jung recorded this passage through the psyche's deepest realms in his masterwork, *The Red Book*, which remained a privately held text until its publication in 2009.

One can read *The Red Book* as an extended, revelatory encounter with Abraxas, who appeared to Jung in the persona of Philemon, an elderly angel who explained the universe's binary truth. For instance, here is Philemon's explication of one of the sacred trees of Eden:

> But he who accepts what approaches him because it is also in him, quarrels and wrangles no more, but looks into himself and keeps silent. He sees the tree of life, whose roots reach into Hell and whose top touches Heaven. He also no longer knows differences: who is right? What is holy? What is genuine? What is good? What is correct? He knows only one difference: the difference between below and above.... Hence he knows the way to salvation.

Jung believed that when we transition from one life stage to the next, we encounter archetypal images from the collective unconscious – the shadow, anima, animus, and the Self in all their forms. These archetypes, with all of their positive and negative manifestations, spring from Abraxas. Therefore, just as Emil Sinclair was passing from adolescence to young adulthood when he discovers Abraxas, and Jung was passing from young adulthood to maturity when he has his vision of Philemon, I was transitioning from maturity to old age when Abraxas arose in me, taking on the forms of darkness and light – a raven and an osprey, a concealed instrument of science and an ancient river glowing in the sun.

V

We woke inside the pyramid enveloped in golden light.

The room was warm, and our lips tasted lightly of salt. From far off, the sounds of children swimming in the hotel pool filtered through the door. It was a liquid sound, as if our pyramid were underwater and not in a high desert valley.

To the southeast, beyond the window, the sun had cleared Sandia Mountain, its great hump a bear's hunched back frozen in stone. Perfectly aligned with the window, the solar orb had set the room ablaze. Though we gazed at the light, we thought only of the gentle pressure of our bodies.

Hours later, when the sun had crossed the sky and hovered over the extended volcanic mounds of the Jemez range, we drove north in the butter-orange sunset through a series of ancient villages – Algodones, San Filipe, Santo Domingo, Peña Blanca, and Cochiti – places of stone and adobe dwelling by centuries-old cottonwood trees with great trunks and branches dense with round green leaves. Outside of Cochiti, just before leaving the verdant Rio Grande to cross the saltbush plains and ascend La Bajada's basaltic cliffs, we got out of the car and stood under one of those cottonwoods while a mild wind blew down from the canyon carved Jemez slopes, and the leaves shifted in the breeze, sounding like water flowing over rippling shallows.

It was a day born in beauty and completed in beauty, as we followed the path of an invisible North Star.

VI

I was walking along a grass-covered dirt road that runs between one of the many branches of the High Line Canal of the Grand Valley and the Colorado River. To my right, the canal moved sluggishly, its brown waters rimmed by algae and rotting cottonwood branches. Occasionally, a river rat would scurry along its muddy banks or slide through its opaque surface, drawing the attention of my dog, Myla, a dachshund-terrier mix, descendant of the planet's best vermin-chasers. To my left, there was a small lake bounded by cottonwoods, tamarisk, and Russian olive trees with blue-green leaves that echoed the sky's color. Out on the lake, a half-dozen herons stood poised to spear fish with their long, pterodactyl bills, and small clusters of Canada geese drifted in the early morning sunlight. Out of sight, beyond the lake, the Colorado River slid over rocks and sand towards the far-off Sea of Cortez.

It was late summer, and the air hummed with cicadas, grasshoppers, golden dragonflies, and the occasional mosquito. Myla, deep chested but a bit low to the ground for a terrier, darted along, thrusting her sharp nose under logs and tangles of dead branches in her search for lizards.

An egret, its impossibly white body sharply etched by the sun, flew over our heads and landed gracefully in the lake.

Then, upon reaching the line of cottonwoods that rise up between the road and the lake, I spotted the osprey.

At the road's end, where a sharp bend in the Colorado River slices off a steep dirt bank, there rests a dead cottonwood, one white truncated branch rising in the air. On that branch the osprey perched, its hawk-like body nobly set against the blue-green Russian olive trees beyond.

I slowed my pace, but kept approaching. When I first spied it, the osprey appeared about the size of my extended thumb. But as we drew closer, the bird revealed its true, intimidating size, nearly as large as a golden eagle. It was eyeing me as I approached, its stabbing beak and precise aerodynamic head in profile. Oblivious to its presence, Myla hunted through the leaves and debris along the exposed cottonwood roots. I began to worry about her, for the osprey was certainly large enough to view my terrier as prey. Still I approached, drawn by the osprey's power and beauty.

Finally, when I was about a dozen paces away, the osprey rose before me, its massive brown and beige wings flexing against the air, its bright, looming body illuminated by the pagan sun. As it ascended into the blue sky, it gave one, eerie, high-whistling call. Even Myla looked up as the osprey passed over us, a vital goddess searching for prey, a sacred embodiment of the cycle of life.

VII

And then the world turned again – the dark into the light into the dark once more – for above, waiting to share in the life the osprey would slay, a pair of ravens circled, laughing at the earthbound mortal beneath them, caught in the universe's dualistic play.

ANGELS OF BONE

"What I am going to describe is strictly illegal," Frederico said. "But far out, away from the authorities, it is still done."

We were sitting under the dim stars of a night sky partially obscured by the glowing clouds of Golden, Colorado. Before us stood a high, round mountain, a giant "M," ringed by lights, emblazoned on its side. Tiny cars, like dark ants with headlights, crawled up the mountain's slopes – teenagers driving up summit to party, make love, and escape the social confines of their age.

The five of us sitting at the picnic table were a good twenty years past such adventures. We had just finished a fine dinner of spiced beef, beans, avocado salad, and rice prepared by our hosts – Frederico Cordovez and Luisa Fernanda.

Short, bearded, and passionate, a delightfully tough geniality possessed Frederico. On the other hand, Luisa – tall, dark haired, and graced by a gentle face and spirit – was like a calming saint. Next to her lounged Katia Forns-Broggi, her hair as dark as Luisa's, but with olive skin and fine, sharp features. Katia was eight months pregnant, and her belly swelled like a full moon. Her husband, Roberto, was uncorking our second bottle of Cabernet. With his dark skin and close cropped hair and beard, he looks Pakistani, though his ancestry is strictly Mediterranean.

We were in a languorous, after dinner mood, and inspired by the wine, our conversation had wandered through many subjects. My companions, all from Latin America, spoke in Spanish and accented English. Frederico was describing the world of the Chileans who live far from the cities, deep in his nation's rugged outback and free from police interference.

"Out there, when a child is born, the midwife will announce to the waiting family that it is either a boy, a girl, or an angel."

"An angel?" I asked.

"Yes. You know, if the child is dead, the belief is that it is innocent, free of sin, so it goes straight to heaven. It is actually a cause for celebration, great parties with lots of drinking."

"I suppose there's some sense to that."

"But that is not the point, not at all. You see, they do not bury the child, not right away. They dress it in white, attach wings, and sometimes even prop open the eyes with toothpicks. Then they place the child in a box and display it, sometimes for weeks – the angel of their family."

Katia nodded. "They do this in Peru also. I have a friend whose father owned a big estate, a *hacienda*, with many workers. My friend, however, went to a boarding school in England, so she spent most of her life away from her home and its customs. Now, imagine this – a few weeks after her return, there was a stillborn child at the *hacienda*, and as the daughter of the *haciendado*, she was expected to attend the funeral. She goes to the home, and there are all these people, drinking and celebrating, which is odd enough. But as she moves amongst them, she starts to wonder about the coffin. She can't find it. At last, she asks, 'where is the child?' And a man points, saying, 'Up there, an angel.' So she looks up, and there, hanging from the ceiling by ropes, is the infant dressed up as an angel, cloth wings and all."

"Fascinating," Luisa said. "I've never heard of this. Maybe they don't do it in Columbia."

"Yes. Strange, isn't it?" added Roberto. "I know of this practice. It definitely happens in Peru, way off in the remote villages."

I, of course, said nothing.

~~~

When my son Nicholas was born, the midwife offered to let me hold him. At first I refused. But just before they took him away for final preparations, I broke down weeping and held out my arms. His tiny, wrinkled face reminded me of my grandfather's. Bundled in white and wearing a miniature knit cap, he looked like an old, fat-faced sailor. He was perfectly still, and, naturally, his eyes were closed.

Later, the nurses returned him to us, not costumed as an angel, but more like a mummy – totally wrapped in white cloth from head to feet. We took him home this way, where he rested for several hours on the kitchen table while I made the arrangements for the burial. My wife, Patricia, lay on the bed, surrounded by several friends who gently massaged her and gave her comfort. There was no celebration.

Later, as the sun slid towards the low, soft mounds of New Mexico's Jemez Mountains, we buried my son with quiet songs and ceremonies, holy blessings and tears. He lies now amidst piñon and juniper, on the slopes of Sun Mountain outside of Santa Fe. Before burial, we covered him in an old Navajo baby blanket, placed his head to the east, and surrounded him with sacred objects. We never unwound hospital's white shroud, so the only time I saw his face was that brief moment I held him before the nurses took him away.

≈≈≈

On the tenth anniversary of Nicholas' death, Patricia and I, along with our daughters Ursula and Isadora, made a pilgrimage from our home on Colorado's Western Slope to his place of burial. As we stood around his grave – which is covered in offerings of colorful stones, crystals, brass bells, beads, a jar of fine black Snake River sand, and a clay Toltec pot a thousand years old – Patricia and I explained to our daughters that their brother was a spirit dwelling everywhere around us; that he is in the air, in the quartzite rocks scattered across the ground, in the piñons and junipers that encircle the site.

Isadora, who was five, found this idea especially impressive, and pondered it for the rest of the trip. On the way home, we stopped for a break not far from the city of Gunnison, in the Cochetopa Canyon – a place of cool waters, green moss, big spruce, and some of the world's oldest granite. It is a profound realm of deep time. Remembering events from ten years past, I stood watching the clean, clear water of Cochetopa Creek surge through rounded gray boulders shot with crystal lace. While her older sister studied a patch of lichen with a new magnifying glass just purchased in Santa Fe, Isadora held my hand in silence, her hazel gaze caught by the dancing sunlight reflected in the curling stream, her short blond hair ruffled by breezes, her round face held captive by serious thoughts.

Suddenly, she broke the silence with her high, clear voice. "Daddy, is Nicholas here with us now?"

"Yes, in spirit."

"Invisible?"

"Yes."

"Is he in the water?"

"Yes."

"The air? The sunlight?"

"I believe so."

And on it went – the earth, the moss, the oak leaves, the spruce needles, the rocks, the cliffs – an affirmation that Nicholas was everywhere, watching over us in silent rapture, hovering in the very wave pulse of light across the matrix of space. And when the litany was complete, Isadora seemed content, and we climbed back into the car to complete our journey.

≈≈≈

The day after my supper at Frederico's, I was heading back to the Western Slope when I stopped in Glenwood Canyon. I hiked down to the Colorado River, where it flows deep, bending through beige and black rock cliffs. I found a large, flat rock standing just up from the river's edge, and sitting upon it I studied the rippling brown water smashing against truck sized boulders. The river sounded like crashing surf, the blue sky was cloudless, and the powerful sun seemed to illuminate the entire universe, except for the caves across the river. As I stared into their shadowy recesses, I thought about infants transformed into angels, of tiny bodies of flesh and viscera and bone hanging from the ceilings of Peruvian homes, and of my own son buried under New Mexican sand and rock. I pondered too on what I had told Isadora several months before in another black rock Colorado canyon. Was it true, I wondered. Or was it just a child's fantasy? Were those peoples living in the remote Chilean and Peruvian highlands correct in their vision? Are their dead infants literally angels with fine spun cloth wings? Or are they vainly trying to make literal a merely sentimental spiritual vision?

At that moment, a heron, like an immense airplane with a heart instead of an engine, began to circle the river. I watched, relieved to find a distraction from my dark thoughts. It landed at last in the shallows on the far bank, barely rippling the water as it settled down. Standing with head cocked, it looked almost ridiculous on its impossible, bone-thin legs. After maybe ten minutes its head darted into the water, and it speared a small fish, a wriggling bit of sunlit silver. Soon after, a monarch butterfly danced past, searching the purple thistle flowers for pollen, followed by the whirring, violent flight of a male hummingbird, plumage iridescent in the sun, the warrior bird of the Aztecs. Above, slate green cliff swallows soared and dived above the river's abyss, catching mayflies by the thousands.

Life and death, I thought, the eternal round of birth and dissolution and rebirth, life consuming life and all undergoing an eternal metamorphosis. I realized then that I had spoken truly when I proclaimed to Isadora that Nicholas dwelled everywhere around us, and the Peruvians were right to deify their deceased infants as angels hovering in heaven, with or without their fabric wings. I knew this because the river had reminded me that all material forms are but masks of eternity, and the form that was briefly my son had dissolved into all forms, just as the waves crashing on the river's boulders soon lose their individual identity to merge with the river's totality. As a coal train began to make its low growling sound up the canyon, a sound so much like distant thunder, I heard my son's voice; and as the wind stirred the dark green cottonwood branches and cooled my face, I felt my son's comforting touch; and as I looked up, I thought I saw my son's fat sailor face and mummy body soaring towards the sun on feathered wings.

In actuality, it was the heron, vanishing into the pure blue sky. But I knew, like those remote Peruvians with their infant angels, and my daughter with her childhood wisdom, that nothing in the universe is truly lost, and what I had momentarily perceived in that heron was a true vision of a reality that dwells far deeper than feathers and bone, skin and blood.

The Carnival Journey

I could see it from my front yard, down there on the river bank where the land was flat and smooth and lined with cottonwoods. The Ferris Wheel, a great mandala of electric lights, turned majestically in the cool desert night. Next to the wheel, twin rockets spun on a steel axis, rapidly pursuing each other in their circumscribed heavens. The rattle of a miniature roller coaster drifted across the plain, along with the clanging of bells and the screams emerging from the more extreme rides, all of it faint with distance.

This was the carnival that arrived magically every year on my daughter's birthday in Delta, a small ranching town in western Colorado. While she was dreaming inside the century-old white clapboard house about the past day spent riding the floating teacups, the merry-go-round's cherry red horse, and the three-story slide, I was outside, watching the distant, spinning lights, remembering carnivals past.

≈≈≈

When I was a child, the carnival showed up every year too, but not on my birthday, since no carnival would ever do business in upstate New York during February, a time when rivers freeze as hard as Arctic iron and ice sheaths the bare branches. Instead, my childhood carnivals occurred in the soft summer nights of June or July, when the oaks and maples are rich in foliage, and the Owego River runs low and slow through Newark Valley, the rural town I lived near until I started college.

And yet, while these carnivals did not appear on my birthday, several did arrive during important transformational periods of my life, and continue to do so. According to Carl Jung, when we go through major personal shifts, both internal and external, we ride our dreams and waking fantasies into the realm of the collective unconscious, where we encounter archetypal figures that help us complete our current metamorphosis. A number of times when I was undergoing a pivotal change, a carnival provided the outer imagery that manifested the mythological symbols stirring within me, much like the mysterious Magical Theater in Hermann Hesse's *Steppenwolf,* which reflects the inner world of the novel's main character, Harry Haller, a seeker of truth in the cabarets of Weimar Germany.

One of the carnivals that fulfilled this role took place the summer after I turned thirteen. At that time, I was becoming acutely aware of my sexual energies. Also, just before then, I had been in several fights at school with a tall, muscular hill-country teen who took an intense dislike to me for, as far as I could tell, no reason whatsoever. Altogether, I was in quite an emotional stew.

As usual, the carnival was the main feature of the Firemen's Field Days, an annual event that raised money for the local volunteer fire departments. That year, the Field Days were being held at the Trout Ponds, a park at the edge of Newark Valley. Lying at the bottom of a small bluff, the park consisted of a stream, rolling green lawns, and several small lakes surrounded by groves of ash, maples, and sycamores.

That year, my father and I went to the Field Days on a Saturday night, and as we drove down the tree-lined road leading to the Trout Pond, I could just make out the carnival, with its game booths, Ferris Wheel, merry-go-round, and other rides, their lights turning and shining in the darkness behind a maze of leaves and branches. The sight made a deep impression on me. I had recently become an avid reader of Ray Bradbury's fiction, and so the carnival had different connotations for me than say three years earlier, when my excitement grew from the rides and the chance to win a giant stuffed giraffe by throwing red wooden balls at stacked white clubs. Now the carnival held the promise of magic and adventures in the realms of the bizarre. I half expected that Mr. Dark from Bradbury's novel *Something Wicked This Way Comes* would show me the world's most beautiful woman in her glass coffin, or the Illustrated Man would order me to gaze at the blank spot on his fabulously tattooed body and I would see my tragic future. As it turned out, I did indeed have an adventure, though it had little to do with Bradbury's shadowy phantasms.

When we reached the bottom of the bluff, my dad parked the station wagon and we entered the carnival grounds. With a squeeze to my shoulder, and a gruffly jovial "have fun," he took off for the fireman's beer tent. In those days, Newark Valley was a "dry" town, and so the sale of alcohol was not permitted. Thus, the firemen's beer tent, exempted from the law as a charitable enterprise, was the closest thing to a local bar Newark Valley ever had. And since it happened only once a year, all those locals who enjoyed the company of fellow drinkers in a public place would gather to seize this rare moment.

Unfortunately, my dad, in order to finish weeding in the vegetable garden, had waited until the light failed to head out to the carnival, so it was already late evening by the time we arrived. The crowds had thinned considerably, and the rides for smaller children – the twirling tea cups, miniature train, and kid-sized army trucks – were all shut down. Wandering the grounds, I could find none of my friends, but I went on several rides anyway. Still, with no one to share the experience, I quickly tired of the Ferris wheel, the whip, and the spinning rockets. A stroll through the rows of carnival booths produced similar results. None of the games of skill pulled me in, even the air rifles, which were my favorite. Indeed, a scattering of booths had already closed.

Finally, feeling restless and bored by the carnival, I wandered off along the stream as it crossed the park grounds. I'm not certain now what drew me on, but the night was certainly magical, with a gibbous moon illuminating the waters as they rippled over a bed of small, rounded shale stones. With distance, even the carnival regained some of its attraction. The garish sounds became muffled, and its gyrating lights grew softer, more mysterious.

Following the stream, I soon entered the forest. The moon lit a faint path that lead deep within, so I quietly left the water to take the trail, which angled off into a tangle of maples, oaks, and ash. The trail began to fade out, but I kept going, the tree trunks becoming wider, the dead leaves thickening underfoot. Beyond the layered matrix of leaves, streetlights from the town at the top of the bluff shone through like mist obscured moons.

Hearing a sound, I suddenly stopped. Off to my right, deeper in the woods, I could just discern two shapes in the dappled moonlight. Curious, I slid through the trees to get a closer look. Within maybe five, six yards, the shapes resolved into entwined arms, naked skin, a torso. Two teens were making love in the forest. She was lying on the leaves, her short skirt bunched up around her thighs. He was still dressed in t-shirt and jeans. As they kissed, he ran his hand slowly up her leg. The scene startled me, but I kept still. From behind me, the muted sounds of the carnival hung on the cool air. The moonlight shifted as the branches creaked in a mild breeze, revealing different aspects of the lovers' movements. The leaves above rustled. The boy and the girl were silent.

Abruptly, I became sharply aware that my presence there was wrong. Without rattling the leaves at my feet, or snapping a dry stick, I shifted my position and walked out of the woods as quietly as a salamander slipping under a stone.

In the time I had been gone, the carnival had wound down even further. The merry-go-round horses stood still in mid-stride, the octopus had ceased its gyrations, the paired rockets hung frozen against the moon-bright sky. Over half the booths were now closed up sleeping clams. Like a hungry ghost, I kept picturing the young lovers in the forest, with their slow movements shifting between clumsiness and grace. Aimless, I wandered up and down the lane of darkening booths and around the soundless, shadow-filled rides. A bitter disappointment at having arrived at the carnival so late set in, and in desperation I set off for the beer tent.

Passing through an entrance formed from rolled and tied flaps, I found a strange and sad echo to the real beer joints my father occasionally patronized in Owego, the nearest "wet" town to Newark Valley. Under the tan canvas roof, about thirty men stood around in clusters of threes and fours, their heads illuminated by a line of bare incandescent bulbs strung across the tent's high ceiling. A makeshift bar formed from an old door set on two sawhorses occupied one of the tent's corners. A squat, balding fellow with a stained apron manned the bar, and past him sat an aluminum keg in a large tin wash-bucket filled with melting chunks of ice. Next to the wash-bucket, five empty kegs marked the day's drinking achievements. A stack of waxed paper cups rested on the bar, awaiting the beer to come.

Next to the bar, a great plywood disc, decorated as a roulette wheel, hung from a wooden platform. As the wheel spun, a series of pegs sticking out from its rim clacked loudly against a wooden flap nailed to the contraption's frame, the staccato sound slowing with the wheel. A cluster of men were gathered in front of a high-legged table facing the wheel. They would take turns placing bets and throwing a set of darts at the wheel, hoping to hit their chosen number and color. The man running the wheel was compact, well-muscled, and wore tight jeans and white t-shirt with a pack of Lucky Strikes rolled up in the sleeve. His blond crew-cut emphasized his sharp features. I recognized him as the assistant scoutmaster of my Boy Scout troop, and almost shouted out a greeting, but I cut it off, realizing this wasn't the time or place to do. Instead, I walked over to my dad, who stood in the middle of the tent's large, open space talking to two friends.

As I walked up, he nodded to me and turned back to his companions, a pair of heavyset men in overalls and work boots. The conversation – all about fertilizer, alfalfa, and crop rotation – quickly lost me. So I watched my father. He had an odd gesture of nodding his round head with quick, short jabs led by his tight, grey mustache. It was his way of indicating assent and encouragement – a mannerism that said, 'Yes, keep going, you're so right.'

After about ten minutes, my father downed the last of his waxed cup of beer and turned to me.

"Done with the carnival?" he asked.

"Yes."

"That was rather quick."

"Well, most of it's shut down."

He nodded. "I'm going to have another beer, and then we'll head for home."

"All right," I answered after a pause. I was hoping we would go right home. The still warm tent smelled of stale beer mixed with sweat, my feet were sore, there was nowhere to sit, and I certainly did not want to hear any more about alfalfa bailing.

While my father and his friends drifted over to the make-shift bar to order more beer, I looked around for some way to kill time. About the only activity in the tent worth watching was the roulette wheel, so I found a spot where I could watch both it and the dart throwers.

The group before the wheel had dropped to three men, and only one of them was throwing. The spectators – two scrawny, denim-clad fellows with bony cheekbones and sharp noses – seemed to be brothers. The thrower, who was downing a lot of beer, was taller, heftier, the angles of his face concealed by puffy cheeks and jowls. He wore a short-sleeved tan shirt and a brand new pair of blue jeans. It cost a dollar to throw three darts, and the buck was the bet – two for one. The thrower was shooting round after round. With every half-dozen sets or so, one of the brothers would run over to the bar and buy the thrower a refill. His eyes were shiny, his stance unsteady.

My assistant scoutmaster was still running the wheel, and even though, like a carnival barker, he was keeping up a stream of encouraging banter, his stance was slouched and his voice had lost its volume and crispness. Clearly, he had been manning the gambling contraption for a long time and was waiting for the long night to end.

But the shooter and his gang were far from done. He had developed a sure-fire method for winning. After declaring his color and number, he would wait for the wheel to slow a bit and then throw the dart with a violent snap of his wrist. The missile would then carve a sharp curve through the air and strike the wheel's outer edge. With this technique, the thrower was hitting his chosen wedge of the wheel nearly three out of four times, and his dollar bills were piling up.

This went on for maybe twenty minutes when the thrower gave the feathered projectile a truly crazy spin. The dart arced wildly through space, sailed past the wheel's edge, and stabbed the wheel spinner in his left thigh.

Abruptly, everything stopped. There was the dart, looking strange and out of place as it projected from the man's leg. The thrower froze, looking shocked and confused. Abruptly, my scout leader's face transformed into an enraged mask as a trickle of blood formed around the dart's metal shaft.

"You son of a bitch," he roared. He lunged for the thrower, but before he could reach him, his leg gave out and he collapsed. The bartender and another man grabbed him under the arms and dragged him past the wheel and out of the tent.

"I'm gonna kill you," he shouted as the tent flaps cut him off from view. "You goddamn bastard!" Muffled by the canvas and the damp night air, it was like a curse uttered from the underworld.

For a moment everyone stared silently at the tent flap through which the wounded man had vanished. Then a babble burst forth – men describing to each other what they had just witnessed. I could hear the shooter declaring in a surprisingly loud and clear voice, "I didn't mean it, I didn't." In a far corner, someone laughed. Meanwhile, my father looked around until he spotted me. Crossing the tent to where I stood in stunned silence, he told me it was time to go home.

All the way back, as the rural blacktop highway rolled into our headlights like some dark river, I kept seeing the girl's bare thighs, the dart sticking from the wounded man's leg, and the small circle of blood forming on his jeans. When we arrived, I went right upstairs to my bedroom. As was usual in the summer, the room was hot despite the open window and the spinning fan, and I had trouble falling asleep. When I did, the night's carnival images shaped the long night's dreams, unleashing the archetypes of sex and violence, creation and destruction, from my deep unconscious.

≈≈≈

Three decades later, I was no longer the child who looked forward to the annual arrival of miniature rides and colorful tents. Instead, it was Ursula, my eight-year-old daughter, who waited in anxious anticipation for the carnival, the one that magically appeared every year on her birthday.

At that time we were living in Delta, a small western Colorado town built on ranches, apple orchards, and sugar beet farms. Of the three, the sugar beet farms had entirely faded away, and where once there had been a series of ponds holding rotting beet husks and other stench-producing waste from the sugar processing plant, there was now a broad lake fed by the clean waters of a Gunnison River tributary and a grassy park with cottonwood trees and smooth lawns. It was here, every year on May 18th, Ursula's birthday, that a travelling carnival would erect its backwater wonderland.

From our front yard we could watch it setting up on the banks of the Gunnison River, past the Southern Pacific rail siding and the grain elevators' twin white towers. It was an especially delightful sight at night, when I would lean against the rough bark of the yard's massive catalpa tree and watch the Ferris wheel make its grand rotation, its spokes outlined by flashing lines of blazing light. I could also see the great disk of a ride called the Flying Saucer, which would heave itself from the ground like a failed rocket launch, spin for a time with red and orange electric fires, and then plunge back to earth. When the cooling breeze blew from the Gunnison, I could just hear the shouts of the riders and the bass thump of the canned rock music.

Usually the day after the carnival had set up, I would take Ursula and her sister Isadora, two years younger, to play in the carnival's magic spaces – with its popcorn vendors, cotton candy weavers, and ring-toss hucksters. And, of course, there were the rides. My daughters were too young to take the truly wild rides, like the colorful steel benches that fling and snap you through the air in frantic, cyclic motions, or the great wheel that spins so rapidly the centrifugal force plasters the rider against the metal walls while the floor drops out. No, the girls, blond and lithe like sky-sprites come to earth to explore the world's delights, would enter instead the carnival's tamer devices – the merry-go-round's plastic horses galloping in a perfect circle to recorded calliope music, the dragon-shaped miniature roller coaster, the fifty-foot high multi-track slide, and the giant metal strawberries that moved in a stately dance. There was even a portable fun-house with stairs that moved from side to side, floor nozzles that startled with sudden bursts of air, a mirror maze, a tilting floor, and a cylinder that tumbled the girls like ragdolls in a slowly turning dryer.

But year after year, their favorite was the Ferris wheel. The best time to take it was at dusk, so that as we rose in the great creaking machine, the silver-painted girders making a clever pattern as they passed on either side, we could look across the western landscape – the dark rise of flat-topped Grand Mesa to the north, the mysterious uplift of the Uncompahgre Plateau to the west, and to the north, the Gunnison River snaking past in the last light, embraced by cottonwoods and Russian olive trees. But the real treat was the array of lights, beginning with the ones on the Ferris wheel itself – long fluorescent tubes in many colors arranged along the wheel's circular grid. Then, surrounding the Ferris wheel, there glowed the carnival's lights – red, yellow, blue, and white, spinning and flying and rotating with their rides. Finally, beyond the carnival lay the lights of the city – the houselights, streetlights, and headlamps of the cars streaming past on U.S. 50, heading for Grand Junction or Montrose or McClure Pass. All of it rising and setting with the stately turn of the wheel, creating a feeling of careful, circumscribed flight.

Ursula especially loved the Ferris wheel, and she would ride it – sometimes with me or her sister, sometimes alone – six or seven times before our night at the carnival came to a close, for she was mesmerized by the wheel's cyclic journey, which landed you back where you started, transformed by delight and a quarter of an hour older.

Nevertheless, the day arrived when Ursula made her final Ferris wheel journey.

She had just turned ten, and was experiencing many significant life changes. Her mother and I were living apart and heading for a divorce. Also, we had moved out of our Delta house with its big glassed-in front porch, its maze of old rooms, its mysterious attic filled with forgotten furniture, and the big catalpa tree from which we could watch the carnival rides blossom across the river flats. Now my daughters and I lived on the ground floor of a small duplex in Grand Junction, a mid-sized city forty miles north of Delta. Still, on the day when Ursula turned ten, we decided to follow tradition and took the trek to the lost world of her birthday carnival.

We drove there on a bright Saturday afternoon, heading south through the shale hills that roll like ocean waves between Grand Junction and Delta. To the east, the basaltic ramparts of the Grand Mesa rose into a blazing white sky. To the west, the sun was a sliced-lemon smear of light behind high, thin clouds. Scattered clusters of antelope stood in the dry, curving spaces, and ravens played in a stiff west wind. This wind worried me as its gusts rocked the car and stirred up dust devils, miniature tornados that tore at the salt brush and sage.

Sure enough, when we reached Delta and turned into the park between the river and the town, the wind was cutting through the carnival, blowing in sand from the arid stretches leading to the Uncompahgre Plateau. Straining to escape, the red and blue and yellow banners snapped in the gale. Many of the concession booths were boarded up, and half the rides were shut down and motionless, machines defeated by the elements. Here and there, groups of sullen teens and blank-eyed families drifted around the nearly empty grounds, seeking something to do.

And yet, to my surprise, the Ferris wheel was running, so we fought our way against the wind to the great steel ring leisurely rotating against the white sky. Scared off by the wind,

Isadora didn't care to get on, so Ursula rode alone. Tall and slender, she carefully placed herself down on the aerial bench, and the operator – a tough, heavyset man in machinist's overalls and grease-stained denim shirt – clicked the safety bar into place across her lap. Back at the controls, he threw a great steel lever and set the wheel ponderously turning. I watched as Ursula rode up into the glaring sky and descended back to earth, a faint smile on her face, her long blond hair whipping in the gale. I pictured what she was seeing as the wheel moved, the town she had called home for seven years dropping beneath her feet and spreading out before her – the riverbank where she had skipped stones, the drug store with its ice cream counter, the century-old brick library where Tin-Tin waited patiently on his shelf, and even, perhaps, a glimpse of the old house and its beloved catalpa tree, its two-story white clapboard structure now occupied by strangers. The wind whistled through the wheel's struts, the gusts rocked the seat back and forth, and the wheel revolved, bringing Ursula visions of her lost world.

Fairly soon, the operator started manipulating various levers, and the great wheel slowed. The journey had seemed shorter than usual. There were only a handful of riders, and Ursula was the last one to get off. After the operator helped her down, he hooked a chain across the gate. Despite this, she held out the right number of tickets to ride again. The operator glanced at her and shook his head.

"I'm shutting down," he said in a gruff voice. "Too much wind."

As if she hadn't heard him, Ursula stood for a time holding out the tickets. Finally, she turned away and stepped down the stairs from the short wooden platform with its closed gateway to the Ferris wheel. Upon joining her sister and me, she still possessed her tight smile, but as we began to cross the half-abandoned carnival, she began to silently cry.

≈≈≈

It would be ten years before we returned to the carnival's sacred grounds, a decade that brought many changes to our lives. I was in a new marriage, and my wife Brenda, who had fully embraced the role of stepmother, was a key figure in helping my now grown daughters navigate the transition from high school to college. It was at this moment of metamorphosis that we made an eight-hundred-mile pilgrimage to a carnival, ending our long exile from its wondrous realm.

I have a cousin in Claremont, one of the many cities that surround Los Angeles like planets circling a massive star. One winter, he and his wife invited all of the descendants of grandfather Nizalowski to spend Christmas Eve at their home in homage to the grand fêtes held on the family farm over forty years ago.

In Polish tradition, the big celebration of Christ's birth is held on Christmas Eve, and the Nizalowski clan followed this tradition in a fine old world manner. The night would begin with the drive from home down a long valley, then up over a forested hill and into a hollow where my grandfather's farmhouse waited, its windows pouring yellow light onto snow-covered fields.

After parking the car and picking up our offerings of food and presents, we passed through a door topped by a spruce bough and entered a place of wonders. Inside, it was all steam and the aromas of good food – cabbage rolls, silvery smelt, mushroom soup, potato dumplings, green beans, and apple pie. Prepared by my mother and my Aunt Jenny, the entire feast was meatless, a Polish custom for the Christmas Eve meal. After setting our covered platters on the kitchen table, there would be the greetings and the long, impatient wait while the final preparations were made.

At last the long living room table would be set, and we entered as if into a shrine. The windows were pure black by now, and as they mirrored the room, the old glass distorted the reflection. Pitchers, bottles, and great platters of food covered the wooden table – a vision of wonder and plenty, a gift directly from the hands of Žytnimatka, the ancient Slavic goddess of grain and the field.

All my relatives on my paternal side, including their spouses and children, took their places at the table, with grandfather Nizalowski at its head. Even though everyone was plenty hungry, there were important rituals to perform before we could eat. My grandfather, tall and wiry in his perpetual bib overalls, and my father, stoutly solid with his neatly trimmed grey mustache and hair, would stand and they would break between them a large, flat rectangle of unconsecrated communion wafer. My grandfather would say a prayer in Polish, and then the two would circle the table while each of us would stand, break off a tiny piece of wafer, and receive a brief kiss on the lips. My father's kiss always felt scratchy because of his mustache. Then we would place the wafer piece on our tongue, feeling it melt away into nothingness.

After this ceremony, the feast would begin – first the mushroom soup, followed by the main dishes. I tended to load up on pierogies, the potato dumplings, because they were my favorite. When I reached my late teens I also took part in the drinking – beer, vodka, and rye in abundance. After the feast, there were Polish Christmas carols to sing, historical subjects to examine, and political arguments to wage. Outside, the moonlight illuminated the snow-draped fields and the bare tree branches afire with frosty crystals. In the barn, according to legend, the farm animals could speak for just one night.

Finally, as the hour grew late, we would shout our farewells, pack the car, and head over the icy hills for the small red-brick Roman Catholic church at the edge of town. Inside, the priest in his finest robes would celebrate midnight mass before a white and gold cloth-covered altar, the whole chapel ablaze with candles and filled with singing voices accompanied by a humble organ.

This is, sadly, a lost world, and our contemporary gathering in southern California could not match it. But we did our best, drinking mulled wine instead of beer and vodka, and eating pesto pasta instead of mushroom soup. But my brother Ed, sister Jean, her son Joshua, and cousin Bob made pierogies according to my mother's beloved recipe, and we sang Christmas carols in both Polish and English, accompanied by Edris, my cousin's wife, on piano; Robert, Edris's son, on guitar; and Isadora, my youngest daughter, on violin. Instead of an icy moon illuminating the snow-draped hills of the Allegany Plateau, the golden sun poured in over the San Bernardino Mountains, setting off flashes of light along the palm leaves and sparking the marigold patches ablaze. And no ice rimed the green lawn.

The day after Christmas, we decided to take a drive to the sea. Our troop of young teens and middle-aged adults piled into two cars and took a freeway west from Claremont, and after an hour we turned onto a two-lane road that climbed a series of switchbacks over the ridge separating Los Angeles from the ocean. As the houses dropped away, the land grew greener, the foliage denser. Now and then, we would pass small ranch houses with unpainted barns and pens with goats, chickens, sheep, and horses – distant echoes of grandfather's farm.

We began to descend a series of tight curves, like the course of an ancient, meandering river, and the cool air that poured through the open windows smelled at last of the sea. About a third of the way down we made an especially sharp hairpin turn, and there it was below us, the Pacific Ocean, a shimmering expanse stretching beyond the western horizon.

At the end of that twisting road, we reached California Highway 1 and turned south. With the sea to our right and the grey coastal cliffs to our left, we drove through a series of gentle, ocean-hugging curves, and then pulled off at one of the many small beaches that line the coast between Santa Barbara and San Clemente. By this time, solid grey clouds covered the sky, and the sun was a wan silvery coin. Despite the chill wind blowing off the sea, we rolled up our jeans, took off our sneakers, and strolled on the wet sand. Pelicans cruised the surf, their wings curled over the crests. Occasionally, one would dive into the surging waters to emerge with a fish. Inspired by the pelicans, Isadora waded waist-deep into the surf to retrieve a piece of driftwood that was about the length and smoothness of her arm, and as blond as her hair. Cheers from her extended family greeted her as she emerged from the sea gripping the stripped branch in her left hand.

With the attainment of this trophy, we all piled back into the cars and continued south, searching for a place to have a fish supper. Several times we stopped at promising possibilities, but every restaurant was either too expensive, too crowded, or lacked indoor seating, and we wanted to get in out of the chilly early evening air.

After several discouraging stops, we came to a bend in the highway where the houses and businesses between us and the sea vanished, and there, in the far distance, all lit up like a gaudy battleship, stretched the Santa Monica Pier, its Ferris wheel and roller coaster ablaze with electric fire. After a quick cellphone conference, we decided to head for the pier, since it would certainly offer an affordable seafood restaurant. I was very excited by this decision, for I had always wanted to visit the Santa Monica Pier, which I've long viewed as the archetypal carnival that stands at the continent's end, like a monument to the gods of amusement. And here we were, serendipitously making the pier the day's final destination.

In 1916, the Santa Monica Pier became the site of an amusement park when German-born manufacturer Charles I.D. Looff created a world-class carnival with roller coaster, arcades, and the Looff Pier Carousel, a 44 horse merry-go-round that operates to this day. The pier park reached its apex in 1924 when its new owners, the Santa Monica Amusement Company, built a titan-sized roller coaster named the Whirlwind Dipper and the La Monica Ballroom, which, at 15,000 square feet, was the largest ballroom in the American West. However, unlike the Looff Pier Carousel, both of these structures are long gone, victims of the pier's declining fortunes, which reached their lowest point in 1983 when severe storms destroyed much of the pier. Fortunately, the people of Santa Monica rallied to save this West Coast icon, and its reconstruction was completed in 1990. Six years later, Pacific Park opened, the first full-scale amusement park on the pier since the late 1930's. And so, the Santa Monica Pier, hovering over the sea like an enchanted city, once more became one of America's most cherished carnivals.

Even though I had never been there, I felt I knew the pier well through certain beloved novels and movies. For instance, in Raymond Chandler's *Farewell, My Lovely*, the character of Laird Brunette runs shuttles from the fictional Bay City to his gambling ship the *Montecito*. Chandler based Brunette on mobster Tony Cornero, who in the 1930's used the Santa Monica Yacht Harbor, which was right next to the pier, to run shuttles to his gambling barge anchored past maritime limits. The scene in which private detective Philip Marlowe prowls the Bay City boardwalk at dusk, preparing to have a confrontation with Brunette in the *Montecito*, is not only a beautiful evocation of the Santa Monica Pier, but is also one of the finest passages in 20th century American literature. And although Ray Bradbury's *Death is a Lonely Business* is set in nearby Venice just days before its pier was torn down, his amusement park descriptions vividly conjure up the Santa Monica Pier in the mid-1940's.

And then there are the movies, like *Night Tide* with Dennis Hopper as a seaman who falls in love with femme fatale Mora, a Santa Monica sideshow attraction mermaid played by Linda Lawson. Or *They Shoot Horses, Don't They?* with Bruce Dern and Bonnie Bedelia, who play a desperate couple participating in a Depression era marathon dance held in the deteriorating La Monica Ballroom. And best of all is *Quicksand*. Set against the pier's arcade and rides as they appeared in 1950, this film noir features Mickey Rooney as a garage mechanic who inexorably slides into a life of crime.

These novels and films were running through my mind as we drove towards the pier and found a place to park. A short walk, and we stepped off the street and onto the pier, past the magical sign that reads: "Santa Monica – U.S. 66 – End of the Trail." Raymond Chandler, Ray Bradbury, John Steinbeck and *Grapes of Wrath*, Jack Kerouac and *On the Road*, "Get Your Kicks" – it all ends here, on the pier's worn, grey planks.

The dying light, like a vein of silver shot with turquoise, hovered on the ocean's horizon. Below, on the beach, a scattering of barefoot people with their jeans rolled up still sought joy in the half-lit sand, running from the surf and assembling altars of driftwood to Poseidon.

But we were here to worship the god of carnivals, not the sea. Ahead of us, yellow, blue, and red neon tubes flashed on and off to the rhythm of the surf. We passed incandescent booths of chance – air rifle, ring toss, and clacking roulette wheel. A game arcade spilled electronically produced sounds of angry guns and roaring engines into the hot dog scented sea-salt air. With a clatter of rails, roller-coaster cars soared into a dark space outlined in dazzling lights. And through the great windows of a century-old stucco building, we caught glimpses of the Looff Carousel, with its brightly painted horses and mirror adorned axle, while above, the Ferris wheel turned in its traditional majesty.

Finally, when our hunger got the better of us, we found a fish restaurant run by a Korean family, and we all ordered great meals of broiled shrimp, grilled tuna, breaded cod, fried potatoes, and clam chowder. After finishing, we strolled once more under the newly born California night, and I felt time being focused by the vast, multi-faceted, many colored lens that is the Santa Monica Pier. A half century of my life was manifested on that boardwalk suspended above the sea: my wife, my daughters, my brother and sister and cousin, all those carnivals from the tree-shrouded Fireman's Field Days to Ursula's birthday celebration out there on the Gunnison River flood plain, all of it brought together under the dim stars and glittering lights here at the nation's far western edge. For this was the final carnival, the completed metamorphosis. At the pier's end I could just make out the curling waves' phosphorescence. At my back, the city lights encrusted the hills with uncounted white diamonds and the occasional ruby. It was truly transcendent, the climax of decades.

In the end, as the western horizon settled into complete darkness, my wife slipped her arm in mine, and followed by my teenage daughters, we began the final walk back to our waiting car. My carnival journey was complete.

Nights at the Burnt Horses

When I moved to Santa Fe in the autumn of 1986, I lived in a one-room apartment with my then wife Patricia just off Park Avenue, a street that bore absolutely no relation to the one in New York City. While it was a lovely space – with pure white stucco walls and an oval, Taos oven style fireplace – it was very cramped with the two of us and the many boxes of books and clothes that our relatives had shipped to us from back east. So to escape the confining clutter, we spent a lot of time outside the apartment.

My favorite refuge was the Burnt Horses Bookstore.

At that time, it was located on Johnson Street, a narrow lane only two blocks long that ran behind the Hotel Eldorado, its massive Pueblo Revival walls looming up like some windowless medieval fortress. Rather austere, the Johnson Street Burnt Horses Bookstore consisted of three modest-sized, well-lit rooms lined with shelves packed with the finest poetry and prose. It also featured a superb Southwestern section. In one room there stood a small, circular table with a few randomly placed slender volumes of poetry. In the main chamber, there were two stuffed armchairs, a combination desk and counter, and a humble wood panel door leading to the street.

Burnt Horses was a pleasant place to spend hours learning about Southwestern literature by reading say Frank Waters' *The Man Who Killed the Deer* or William Eastlake's *Portrait of an Artist with Twenty-Six Horses* for the first time. Also, the owner, Robert Hayes, was a great conversationalist who knew literature and Southwestern culture inside and out. Tall, bearded, and looking like an extra from the film version of *A River Runs Through It*, Hayes was a

Montana native who had stopped short of getting his Ph.D. to open a bookstore in New Mexico. Many an afternoon I would journey to Downtown Subscription Coffeehouse in the Burro Alley courtyard, buy a double espresso, take it to Burnt Horses, and hang with Robert, talking about everything from the New Mexican novels of Conrad Richter to Anasazi ruins to fly fishing.

Occasionally, I would stay through to the evening and attend one of the many readings there. This was how I encountered the poetry of John Knoll, who lived in an old wood-frame house surrounded by cottonwoods about thirty miles north of Santa Fe near the San Ildefonso Indian Pueblo. A wonderful surrealist poet of the first order, Knoll was a tall, slouching man with a rather dour Germanic face who would perform his pieces with all the passion and theatricality of a modern prophet. This was also where I met David Seals, who read from his comic novel *Powwow Highway*. He was in Santa Fe to be a technical advisor on the novel's film version, which was being shot just blocks away in the plaza. Seals was a gregarious, overgrown cherub, and he hung with the audience after the reading, telling wonderful stories about the misadventures of film-making.

Before too long, I started working for Robert as one of his part-time clerks. He paid us $5.00 an hour, which was just above minimum wage in 1986. That was all he could afford since the book business can be a very perilous operation, especially in Santa Fe with its absurdly high rent. And yet, all his clerks had a least a B.A., and some had Master's degrees. For a time, he even had an employee with a Ph.D. While this says something about the crazy competitiveness for jobs in Santa Fe, it is also an indication of how wonderful it was to work for Robert at the Burnt Horses Bookstore. It was one of the finest jobs I've ever had, and while I went through a mixture of full and part-time positions in Santa Fe, I kept my job at the Burnt Horses throughout my New Mexico sojourn.

Soon after I started working at Burnt Horses, Patricia and I moved to a small, two-bedroom adobe about three blocks from the plaza. Burnt Horses moved also, to East De Vargas, the oldest street in Santa Fe, indeed the oldest in the United States. Robert teamed up with a woman who planned to open a restaurant, and Burnt Horses became the Burnt Horses Bookstore and Nighthawk Café. While most businesses in Santa Fe closed by 6:00 p.m. and many restaurants by 9:00 p.m., Burnt Horses stayed open until midnight, and this only increased its magic and its importance. Indeed, it was during its De Vargas Street era that the Burnt Horses became the center for Santa Fe's literary scene.

At first, I walked to my evening shifts at the Burnt Horses, and I relished the passage home after midnight, when the streets were empty and my footsteps would echo off the ancient adobe walls of the Palace of the Governors. Even though the darkened galleries were closed, the streetlamps lit the paintings behind the plate-glass windows as if to give me a private nocturnal showing.

But when my next-door neighbor, a jazz drummer, got knifed while coming home from a late gig at the La Fonda Hotel, I decided that I better stop walking to the bookstore. So, a typical evening's work at Burnt Horses would begin with a dash across the city's old quarter in my rusty machine-red 1969 Toyota Land Cruiser. Careening around the corner of Old Santa Fe Trail and East De Vargas, roaring like an enraged Minotaur, that Land Cruiser scattered tourists like chickens and devoured the street's peaceful, timeless atmosphere.

I used to start my evening shift around suppertime, and there would be a steady stream of people passing through the bookstore to reach the attached restaurant. The bookstore clerk's desk sat squarely in the center of the space, bookshelves all around, with another, smaller room behind it also lined with books. To the left, a large rectangular opening lead to the Nighthawk Café. Therefore, the whole Santa Fe night parade passed before us in fantastic array. Wealthy patrons dressed in sharply creased khaki, turquoise bolo ties, and Stetson hats mingled with aging hippies in worn jeans and soft pastel shirts. Drinking cold bottles of Tecate, Los Alamos technicians off "The Hill" murmured about "dumping the stuff in the canyon" before drifting towards the back room to discuss their classified problems in greater secrecy. Eighties bohemians in stud-obsessed black leather jackets would grab espressos from the café and slouch in front of the poetry section thumbing through the latest Jim Carroll volume.

The climax of the nightly cavalcade usually arrived around 10:00 p.m. with a man in his thirties I'll call Zack. For a long time I thought Zack was the king of the street people. He would always enter leading an entourage of homeless men – three or four guys with stained grey overcoats, tangled hair, and pale bearded faces. Zack was probably five-foot-two and had a pug's face with a perpetual three day's growth of beard. No matter the weather, he always wore a wool army jacket the color of dried mud and an army surplus fur cap with earflaps. And stink. You could smell Zack the moment he entered the shop. I swear he took baths on a bimonthly basis.

Upon arrival, Zack would seek out the most attractive, sophisticated woman in the place and pursue her from one room to the next while murmuring a stream of sexual come-ons in a raspy, high-pitched voice. Usually he would let up after the woman uttered a virulent insult or two, but occasionally we had to call the police to eject him back into the New Mexican night. When he wasn't shadowing women, he obsessed about conspiracy theories. He claimed that Queen Elizabeth was the number one heroin exporter to the United States, Stephen King engineered the murder of John Lennon for the CIA, and the author of *The Satanic Verses* purposely wrote the novel to be under fatwah because his name was Salmon "Rush Die," with the stress on the second syllable.

One night, while Zack was in the Nighthawk Café harassing the wait staff, his chief lieutenant – a tall, lanky fellow who somehow managed to stay clean-shaven – stood by my desk. He glanced towards the archway between the restaurant and the bookstore, and then bent down towards me.

"I bet you think Zack lives in the street, eh?"

"Well," I said, wondering what this was all about. "Sure."

"He actually has a decent apartment. He lets me sleep there now and then, when things get too dicey along the Santa Fe River.'

"Where does he get his money?"

"His dad's a big-time investment banker in Chicago. Zack got sent down here cause he's too weird for home."

"Well, yes, I can certainly understand that."

"Yeah, well, Zack has an antique coin collection worth thousands of dollars. Every so often he sells a coin and we all get to eat good for weeks."

I must have looked skeptical, because the lieutenant spat out, "You ask him. God damn it, ask him to show you his coins. Just ask him." And he stalked off to a shelf in the far corner, burning the black and white spine of the Vintage Press edition of James Joyce's *Ulysses* with his pale blue eyes.

So a few nights later I asked Zack about his coin collection. He grinned his evil little grin and nodded.

"Yeah – I got coins. Roman mostly. I've got one in my pocket I'm thinking of selling. Wanna see it?"

"Sure."

And he took out a dirty bronze object that nicely covered his inner palm. An imperial head gazed somberly towards the coin's sinister side, some sort of Latin phrase circumambulating the outer rim. When Zack picked it up and turned it over, the other side bore a warrior with a spear and shield facing dexter, bracketed by the letters 'S' and 'C.' I was certainly impressed.

"How much does a coin like that go for?"

"It's not especially rare. May fifty, sixty bucks."

After seeing the coin, I had a far different understanding of Zack and his world. Instead of living under a bridge on Alameda, he was a wealthy eccentric who embraced street life by choice. He was one of Santa Fe's many strange characters – like the long-haired clarinetist who played atonal midnight jazz atop the hill by the Cross of the Martyrs or Tommy Macaione, the old bearded artist who painted every day in the small triangular park by East Marcy Street. These were the kind of oddly fascinating denizens who helped make Santa Fe an intriguing place that attracted poets and writers, and these authors made Burnt Horses a literary center by doing readings, buying books, and sketching out poems and stories at its tables while the afternoon sun streamed through its dusty rectangular windows.

Though it is better known for its artistic scene, Santa Fe possesses a rich literary tradition.

Santa Fe acquired its literary pedigree in 1880 when the territorial governor of New Mexico, Lew Wallace, released his epic novel *Ben Hur*, and the archeologist Adolf Bandelier, who had been exploring the Anasazi ruins in the nearby Jemez Mountains, published his novel of ancient Pueblo Indian life, *The Delight-Makers*.

Then, in 1917, Santa Fe became a literary capital when Alice Corbin-Henderson, associate editor of *Poetry* and a close friend and supporter of Carl Sandburg, moved to the city to heal from tuberculosis. She in turn attracted Witter Bynner, who in the early 20th century was one of America's major poets. Inspired by the ancient capital's remarkable blend of colonial Spanish and American Indian cultures, Bynner and Henderson generated a literary colony that rivaled Greenwich Village, Martha's Vineyard, Carmel, and nearby Taos. By the mid-1920's, Santa Fe had become the home of novelist Willa Cather, essayist Mary Austin, poet Haniel Long, and playwright Lynn Riggs. Such luminaries as D.H. Lawrence, Vachel Lindsey, Thornton Wilder, Edna Ferber, and Robert Frost visited for extended periods. Over the decades, a steady stream of poets and writers would land in Santa Fe and continue building its literary heritage, from Pulitzer Prize novelist Oliver LaFarge in the 1930's to Native Writers Circle Lifetime Achievement Award winner Joy Harjo in the 1970's.

When I lived there in the late 1980's, Santa Fe's literary scene continued to flourish. It was incredible how many writers one could encounter crossing the plaza or strolling up Canyon Road.

J.R. Humphreys, with his wild white hair and Guatemalan knitted sweater, might be sipping spiced tea at an outdoor table at Downtown Subscription, while fellow novelist John Thorndike, his face set in a slender, preoccupied smile, would enter the shop to purchase the latest *Paris Review*. Meanwhile, out past Paseo de Peralta, elderly Richard Erdoes, author of *Lame Deer, Seeker of Visions*, sat slim and stooped in his wood-paneled house regaling a young journalist with his astonishing story of fleeing Berlin while on the Nazi death list for anti-fascist activities. Science-fiction writer Roger Zelazny, his bony, intelligent face pensive in the dying light, would be peering out from his home's front picture window, studying an especially colorful sunset over the Jemez Mountains. Later, when the sun was long gone over the earth's rim, Zelazny's friend George R.R. Martin, wearing his signature Greek sailor's cap and looking like an overgrown bearded gnome, would stand in the doorway of Club West, watching the 60's L.A. band Spirit play "Nature's Way." The next morning might find essayist Frederick Turner, a New England scholar who had fled to the Wild West, studying with disapproval the over-priced art along East Water Street, while several blocks away, short-story author Jocelyn Lieu edited the *Bienvenidos* section at the offices of the *Santa Fe New Mexican*, her diminutive form dwarfed by the drafting table. Young-adult novelist Gerald Hausman, long oval face and drooping mustache, also worked at editing tasks, though his were at the offices of Lotus Books. Not far, bearded *cuentos* writer Jim Sagel studied with sad eyes the traditional Nuevomexicano weavings hanging in an Ortiz Street shop, his suicide in a Rio Grande *bosque* a decade away.

And poets. In the 1980's, Santa Fe possessed poets in great abundance, some of the finest in the nation. Mei-Mei Berssenbrugge and Arthur Sze might be silently composing elegant verse in their heads while sipping jasmine tea under the afternoon's silvery light, the Galisteo Basin arrayed before them with its meandering cottonwood wrapped rivers and its ancient cities buried under desert sands. Or bearded Christopher Merrill, with his curious mixture of affability and deep intention, expounding excitedly about his new forays into creative non-fiction, the horrors of the Balkan War, which he will write about in *Only the Nails Remain*, still years in the future. Tall, aristocratic Alvaro Cardona-Hine, with silver goatee and hair, descending from his home in the Sangre de Cristo Mountains like some Renaissance prophet. Leo Romero, bewhiskered like a colonial Spanish monk, performing his sharply humorous Celso poems in stoic deadpan to a delighted audience. Robert Winson, looking like a slender version of Leo Romero, shouting his raging Zen verses alongside a punk band, with his wife, Miriam Sagan, the poetic reincarnation of Emma Goldman, smiling benignly from a front row seat. Harold Littlebird, his face like a warm sun, sitting in a diner over eggs and coffee joyously telling stories of travelling the country on the Santa Fe Railroad with his father, a rail worker from Santo Domingo

Pueblo. Gregory Waits – tall, slender, performance poet from Chicago chanting in his sonorous voice, "The Grail, we're all searching for the Holy Grail." The St. John's College poets – lofty intellectual Charles Bell, who had been friends with Albert Einstein and J. Robert Oppenheimer, and Jorge Aigla, the brilliant physician-poet from Mexico and former San Francisco city coroner. And welcoming us all into his just constructed mansion in the Tesuque Hills, there would be Victor di Suvero, who possessed all the old world charm of an Italian Duke.

These and other New Mexican writers would often appear at the Burnt Horses Bookstore to do readings, and their frequent performances helped make the shop the center of literary Santa Fe. Being one of the Burnt Horses clerks, I would set up and MC for many of these readings, and this was one of the delights of the job. Still, of the more than one hundred creative presentations I witnessed at the Burnt Horses, there were three that truly stand out.

Matthew Robertson, a New Zealander who married an American film documentarian, landed in Santa Fe about a year after I did. He was one of the finest performance poets I have ever encountered. His verses were rooted in 60's era surrealism and his acting style descended from Davie Bowie. Blond-haired and bony, he often wore colorful masks with stylized stars and clouds and lightning that were works of art. He also used props, everything from an air-horn to a plastic sheep model. Tape loops and a rhythm machine completed Robertson's scene.

Another brilliant Santa Fe performance poet was Mateo Galvano. He has since gone on to concentrate on painting and installment pieces, but back in the 80's, he focused on poetic and theatrical presentations. At one reading, he stood before us with his bushy blond hair and composed angel's face, wearing a white short-sleeved tunic. Beside him, a small table held a clear glass vase with a half-dozen irises and a large pair of black-handled scissors. Then, while he recited Rilke, he used the scissors to cut up the irises one flower at a time. Just as he completed the poem, he pulled the last iris from the vase and faced momentarily away from the audience. When he turned back, he was slicing his bare right arm with the open scissors. Blood slid from a thin red line. All the time his face remained expressionless. It was a powerful and shocking moment, a kind of theater vérité.

But the finest reading of all was from N. Scott Momaday.

N. Scott Momaday is the author of over ten books of poetry and prose, including *House Made of Dawn*, which won the Pulitzer for fiction in 1969. A large Kiowa man, with a monumental body like an Olmec statue, Momaday has a deep, but sensitive voice that is reminiscent of Orson Welles. In 1990, Momaday had just released *The Ancient Child*, his novel about a Kiowa man who discovers that he is the living incarnation of the Bear Boy, a central figure from Kiowa mythology.

Soon after the novel's publication, Momaday did a reading at the Burnt Horses. Before his appearance, he had us arrange the shop to his specifications. We had a large cream-colored armchair that we turned to face the open, central space where we held the readings. Next to the chair, we placed a standing lamp with a yellow shade. At Momaday's directions, we kept the area in front of the chair clear, and arranged folding chairs in an arc further out, almost to the store's walls. When the audience arrived, Momaday was sitting in the chair, a glass of water on the end table next to him, and a copy of *The Ancient Child* in his right hand. He bid people to sit on the floor around his seat, and most did, but for a number of the older audience members who used the folding chairs. He then asked us to turn out the lights, excluding his standing lamp. The shop was plunged into a shadowy darkness, except for the circle of yellow-tinted light which illuminated his massive figure and the collection of lifted faces gazing up at this genius author.

It was story hour with N. Scott Momaday.

He read various passages from the novel, starting with the Kiowa myth of Tsoai, the great volcanic neck that is Devil's Tower in Wyoming, and continuing with Pat Garrett's assassination of Billy the Kid in 1881. The reading attained the level of true dramatic theater. Then, when Momaday read the passage in which the spirit of Billy the Kid meets the spirit of the great Kiowa chief Set-angya, the author rendered Set-angya's voice with full operatic power. It was like listening to a god speaking out of the depths of mythological time. Billy the Kid he did in a pitch-perfect Texas prairie twang. With Momaday's brilliant writing and superb vocal craft, the spirit world conversation between these two western legends became sharply vivid in our imaginations. Even as I write this account, that fictional encounter of Billy the Kid and Sitting Bull feels more real to me than many of my actual experiences.

Sadly, it seems that we always find ourselves banished from Eden, no matter how hard we try to remain.

Santa Fe was, and still is, a difficult place to live if you don't have money in your background. The jobs pay poorly, even the professional ones, and the rents are at a premium. In 1990, just before Patricia and I left, I was working five different part-time jobs just to tread water. The stress of these efforts was wearing enough, but when our first-born child was stillborn, the shock of his death was genuinely demoralizing. We buried him in the foothills of Atalaya Mountain, southeast of Santa Fe, and somehow the high desert sun, the rolling expanse of juniper and piñon, the maze of adobe lined streets beyond the mountain's curve, no longer seemed worth the struggle to stay. By August, we had moved to Colorado's western slope for a new life in a new world.

Around the same time, there was a bitter break between the owner of the Nighthawk Café and Robert Hayes. The Nighthawk Café owner pulled out and filed a lawsuit against Hayes. To keep the bookstore-café open, Robert hired a young man who had studied fine cuisine in Mexico City and knew how to make over fifty different kinds of mole sauces, but it was to no avail. Within a year of my leaving Santa Fe, the Burnt Horses Bookstore closed its doors for good.

Still, despite being capped by tragedy, the years I lived in Santa Fe remain some of the brightest in my life. The diverse people, the architecture, the artwork, the bookstores, the coffee houses, the deeply rooted American Indian and Spanish civilizations – all blended into a vibrant cultural matrix that nourished my soul. But beyond all of this, there were the many fine writers drawn to live in a place not because of a university position or a publishing job, but because they desired to be there, in Santa Fe, joining a century old literary tradition that continues to this day. Santa Fe in the 1980's was my Paris in the 1920's – my moveable feast. It was in New Mexico that I truly studied the literary craft and found my voice as a writer.

And, finally, there were the warmly lit rows of superb books, the readings, the performances, the rich coffee, the local artwork on the stucco walls, the conversations with fellow writers pursuing the truths of story-telling or versifying – all those timeless, shimmering, and sometimes shadowy nights at the Burnt Horses Bookstore.

ON THE AIR

The attic was hot and dusty. Yet it was a place of wonders.

Over two centuries in age, the house's oldest section, the domain of the attic, stretches back to the 1780's. Hand hewn oak beams run overhead, forming a high peak filled in with wood planks. Not a single nail holds the frame together; instead, thumb-sized wood pegs create bonds and joints. In my childhood years, columns of cardboard boxes, a scattering of dusty rattan chairs, and several battleship gray cabinets filled this space. A single flyspecked window at the attic's west end let in a wan, almost silvery light – except at sunset, when sometimes a golden glow worthy of illuminating the pyramids would pour in through the old wavy glass. Overhead, a single, oversize 150-watt bulb set in a white painted steel reflector usually shed more radiance than the window. Centered under the bulb's bright beam, a wind-up record player sat perched on a dark wood resonator the size of a small cabinet.

That day, the top was propped open, and a 78-rpm record, double the thickness of any modern vinyl album, nestled on the turntable, its dull black center emblazoned with the Columbia label in silver and white. Reaching down, I gripped the wood handle, turned the heavy iron crank on the cabinet's side, and released a simple steel catch that allowed the disc to spin. The whole apparatus stood about chest-high on my ten-year-old body. Looking at my older cousin, I waited for my cue. He held a shiny aluminum cylinder, one of the odd pieces of high-tech trash my father would bring home from his job at the defense plant building missile guidance systems. It was our pretend microphone. Several grades ahead of me, this cousin was tall, gangly, and dark-haired. His fair-haired brother, closer to my age, sat at one of the antique chairs, elbows on knees, chin to cupped palms.

The older cousin, Bob, began to speak in the over-annunciated tones of a 1940's era radio announcer, a voice he'd learned from watching old movies on late night television.

"And now we bring you the great Benny Goodman and his orchestra playing the ever popular, 'Sing, Sing, Sing.'"

Bob pointed to me, and I carefully placed the tone arm – its heavy, circular end holding the shiny steel needle – down on the record. There was the characteristic *skritch, skritch, skritch* of 78's, and then the multi-layer, tight swing arrangement of "Sing, Sing, Sing," driven by Gene Krupa's pounding drums, burst from the sounding box, all muffled and boomy, the high notes skittering like scurrying phantoms.

Now Ray, my other cousin, spoke up.

"Let it play for a few minutes, and then turn it off. Bob, you come in and say, 'we interrupt this program to bring you special news report.'"

"O.K."

We waited, listening to the music of a time before we were born. Someone coughed from the dust – tiny motes that seemed to catch fire when they drifted past the incandescent bulb.

About mid-way through Goodman's clarinet solo, I lifted the tone arm. Despite my care, the needle caught the record, and the sound, like a ripping zipper, made me wince. Right on cue, Bob launched into an announcement straight out of Orson Welles's *War of the Worlds*.

"We interrupt this musical program to bring you this news bulletin from our special correspondent – Raymond Kuzia. And now to you, Raymond."

Bob handed the metal cylinder to Ray, who attempted the deep tones of a stereotypical newscaster. "This just in from the news room. *The Phoebe Snow*, the passenger train that serves our fair city, has run off the rails at the Susquehanna Bridge and plunged to the waters below. Hundreds are feared dead. More on this story at six."

Ray nodded to me, and I placed the needle back on the record more or less where I had interrupted the song. As we listened to the rest of "Sing, Sing, Sing," and then played more of my parents' 78's and made more overly dramatic announcements, the sun slid towards the green hills just past the attic window. But we didn't notice, for time had been magically suspended by one of our favorite games – radio.

≈≈≈

About five years later, my radio game became more real.

My parents' 18th century home was one of the first houses built on the southern end of Brown Road, a rural route that paralleled the Owego River between the upstate New York villages of Berkshire and Newark Valley. On the northern end of Brown Road, my good friend Carl Akins lived in a house that was maybe a century younger, and in his second story bedroom he set up an amateur radio station by purchasing a low wattage transmitter just under the legal power limit for an unlicensed station. Carl's station, which he named WBRS, reached perhaps a half mile radius, but it was real radio, and Carl's neighbors and passing cars on Brown Road or Route 38, the nearest state highway, could tune in our broadcasts, though they rarely did.

But that didn't stop Carl from creating an entire production studio. Next to his bed and wooden chest of drawers, he set up a table with two turntables, a broadcast quality microphone on a suspension stand, a mixing board, an antenna cable that ran up the wall and out the window, and the transmitter – a featureless black box about the size of the Ace paperback edition of Frank Herbert's *Dune*. Along with this equipment, the shelves upon shelves of albums and tangles of multi-colored wires didn't leave much room for visitors. So we would squeeze into Carl's small, sloped-roof bedroom any way we could – sitting on the bed, the chair, or the floor – and spend our Friday's and Saturday's being DJ's by spinning records, announcing songs, and gossiping about the latest bands. Sometimes we would go deep past midnight, huddling under the single desk lamp, while Carl, looking like some elfish character out of a Tolkien novel, would pull record after record from his copious stacks. Like electronic alchemists, we would transform those records into radio waves and send them out to the vast dark beyond Carl's two tiny windows, playing the great music of the day – the Beatles, Doors, Arthur Lee, Yes, Led Zeppelin, Cream, Rolling Stones, Jefferson Airplane, and many, many others. And always there was that magic feeling that there was a real signal going out into space, that someone could actually be listening.

In the final year or two of the station's existence, I gained my driver's license, and I would get a kick out of listening to Carl, still broadcasting as I headed for home on the narrow country blacktop road, my headlights lighting the way ahead with its railroad crossing, white X warning signs, brown barns, white clapboard farmhouse, clusters of maples – all accompanied by say the mysterious tonal soundtrack of Pink Floyd's "Set the Controls for the Heart of the Sun," which would quickly fade out, leaving white noise shot with static as I reached the limits of Carl's transmitter.

≈≈≈

Radio, or at least the concept of radio, dawned in 1873, when the Scottish physicist James Clerk Maxwell predicted that an electric occurrence, say a bolt of lightning or an electric discharge from a battery, should create waves that travel through space in the same manner and speed as light. This is because electrical fields generate magnetic fields, which in turn generate electrical fields, and this dualistic play produces an electromagnetic wave. The trick was to create a device that could detect these invisible waves.

Fifteen years later, Heinrich Hertz created a device that did just this. Hertz set up two small brass spheres hooked to battery powered induction coils. When he engaged the coils, a spark would jump the gap between the spheres. If Maxwell's predictions were correct, the sparks should create electromagnetic waves. To detect these waves, Hertz formed a receiver from a looped wire tipped by brass spheres, a kind of physical echo to the transmitter. The receiver stood several meters from the transmitter. Hertz knew that the electromagnetic waves generated by the transmitter's sparks should induce a current in the wire loop and create sparks between the receiver's brass spheres – a wireless transmission of energy through space. When Hertz turned on the transmitter, this indeed happened. Sparks shot forth between the receiver's spheres in response to the transmitter's discharge of energy. The German physicist was triumphant – he had witnessed the first broadcast and reception of electromagnetic waves, in essence, the first radio transmission.

Following Hertz's discovery, a number of scientists and tinkerers improved on his experiment, so that by 1900 modern radio was a reality. Of these inventors – a partial list includes J. C. Bose, Guglielmo Marconi, and Nathan Stubblefield – by far the most colorful was Nikola Tesla.

The inventor of our Alternating Current (A.C.) system of power transmission, Tesla was obsessed with the wireless broadcast of energy through space. In 1899, he built a laboratory of wonders high in the mountains above Colorado Springs. Here this Serbian-born inventor developed the Tesla Coil, which generated sparks 30 feet long that could be seen ten miles away, and by using the earth as a conductor, he lit 200 electric lamps from a distance of 25 miles without the use of wires. There are bizarre photographs from that lab showing the dapper Tesla sitting in a chair calmly reading a book while torrents of electric discharges break around his head from a massive silver colored ball. One of Tesla's proud-est wonders was the lab's highly sensitive radio transmitter/receiver on which he claimed to have detected signals from the planet Mars, a declaration that brought widespread skepticism and even derision. Today, some historians believe he may have been picking up Marconi's transmitter in Italy, which Tesla mistook for extraterrestrial communications.

Wherever the signals emanate, radio waves are generated by a transmitter that pushes electric charges in a set pattern up and down an antenna. This creates electromagnetic waves – a pair of electric and magnetic fields that weave across space, one eternally producing the other. Upon reaching a radio set, the wave's electric field pushes charges up and down the receiving antenna in the same way that Hertz's wire loop responded to the sparks from his induction coils. To gener-ate sound, the radio transmitter varies the amplitude, or strength, of the wave in a pattern that mirrors the sounds produced in the studio. This amplitude pattern controls the movement of the receiving radio's speaker, and these movements create sound. This is called AM, or Amplitude Modulation. In FM, or Frequency Modulation, the transmitter alters the wave's precise frequency as the means to control the speaker's fluctuations.

In the beginning, radio was used primarily for ship's communications and was essentially restricted to Morse Code. However, improvements in the long-distance transmission of speech inspired the Westinghouse Electric Corporation to establish the first commercial radio station, Pittsburgh's KDKA, in 1920. In just two years, there were 550 radio stations and 1.5 million radio sets, a number that today has reached 33,000 stations and more than two bil-lion radios world-wide.

One of the characteristics of radio that increases its air of sorcery is the nighttime ability of simple receivers to pick up AM signals from hundreds or even thousands of miles away. This seemingly miraculous phenomenon is due to the ionosphere, a layer of the upper atmosphere consisting of charged particles that form when the sun's x-rays and ultraviolet radiation strike molecules of oxy-gen and nitrogen. The lowest layer of the ionosphere, which absorbs AM signals, vanishes at night, allowing the AM radio waves to reach the ionosphere's higher layers 100 miles up. These layers bounce back the signals, enabling them to go far beyond the line of sight limitations of daytime broadcasting. Shortwave radio achieves great distances on the same principle, though some of the frequencies used in shortwave are less affected by the lower ionosphere and can therefore achieve an atmospheric bounce even in daylight hours.

Ernest Hemingway depicts the ionosphere's effect on radio signals in his short-story "The Gambler, the Nun, and the Radio." The story's protagonist, Mr. Frazer, lands in a small hospital in Hailey, Idaho with a broken arm. After five weeks in the hospital, Frazer's insomnia has become almost unbearable. He finds relief in the radio, which he listens to well past midnight as the stations sign off one after another, moving west with the night – Denver, Salt Lake City, Los Angeles, and finally Seattle at five a.m. After Seattle leaves the air, he can pick up Minneapolis starting its broadcast day. He begins to know these cities through their radio stations, especially Seattle with its big white taxicabs that carry passengers escaping prohibition to Canadian roadhouses and Minneapolis with its Morning Revelers, who cart their instruments on the streetcar as they head out to do their morning musical program. Between tracking the nighttime radio signals, listening to the stories of the staff and patients, and the occasional illicit drink, Frazer manages to keep his sanity.

I discovered this long-range AM broadcasting effect around the same age that I began playing radio station in the attic. Sometimes when my father and I would go fishing, we would return home late, and as the country highways wound through the darkened forests and fields, we would tune in to WWVA and the Wheeling Jamboree from Wheeling, West Virginia 300 miles away. So, with the smell of newly caught bass in my nostrils, I would listen to the bluegrass of Doc Williams, Mac Wiseman, and Jim Greer's Mac-O-Chee Valley Folks, punctuated by Crazy Elmer's comedy routines. Because of the radio broadcast's distant origin, it seemed to me as exotic as Tesla's signals from Mars or the mysterious, silent pulse of northern lights on the equinox midnights.

Some thirty years later I frequently experienced the same strange effect. At the time, I was living in Delta in western Colorado, and teaching forty-five miles away in Grand Junction. When I would drive home from my night classes, I would listen to KNX 1070 out of Santa Ana, California, their radio waves vaulting 700 miles over the deserts of the Mohave and the Colorado Plateau to reach me. Every night at ten o'clock Mountain Time, nine Pacific, KNX would play an hour of radio dramas from the 1940's and 1950's. It was as if I were driving a time machine across western Colorado's adobe hills and dry gulches, occasionally catching a coyote or an antelope in the headlights, while listening to Jimmy Stewart as Britt Ponset, the cowboy drifter in *The Six Shooter*, or Bret Morrison in *The Shadow*, piercing the hidden hearts of men; or an interstellar adventure on *Dimension X*, with announcer Norman Rose intoning at the start of every episode – "Adventures in time and space, told in future tense."

I've long been fascinated by the Golden Age of radio theater, and back in the mid-1970's I felt almost a part of it when I wrote "dramatic" radio ads professionally. In 1976, two WBRS announcers – Carl Akins and Todd Rutan – formed a radio production company specializing in ads, and they hired me as their copywriter. Our pitch was that we were the creative radio ad outfit for New York's Southern Tier, and we made mostly 30 second dramatic spots with scenarios like Sherlock Holmes perceiving that Dr. Watson had visited our client's pizza joint because of the doctor's grin of profound satisfaction, or talking fish complaining that ever since a certain scuba diving outfitter had gone into business, the Susquehanna River had become crowded with happy divers. We didn't make a great deal of money, but it was a real kick to be driving around town and hear an ad, complete with characters and sound effects, come over the radio and know that I had written it.

During the years that I wrote ads for Carl and Todd, I exercised my fascination for radio drama on WHRW, the campus station for Binghamton University, where I was working on my B.A. in English. My weekly show was a science-fiction and fantasy program that consisted mostly of playing recordings of old radio plays like Orson Welles's Mercury Theater production of *Dracula* or dramatic readings of classic science-fiction stories like Leonard Nimoy's performance of Robert Heinlein's "The Green Hills of Earth." As with WBRS, there was something magical about sitting in front of a microphone and announcing the show. But unlike the amateur station of my teen years, my voice was reaching an audience in a thirty mile radius, not three hundred yards.

Yet once I graduated from Binghamton, I didn't step into a radio studio for a full decade, and it was poetry, not radio drama that drew me back. In 1986, I moved to Santa Fe, the centuries old capital of New Mexico. In those days there was an active performance poetry community, and the heart of this community was Burnt Horses Bookstore on De Vargas, the nation's oldest street.

Dwelling in a humble single-story brick and adobe structure with seasoned vigas that glowed in the lamplight, Burnt Horses was the locale of numerous readings, sometimes two or three a week. These ranged from marathon open readings with legions of apprentice poets to presentations from literary greats like recording artist John Trudell, who filled the place with black balloons to accompany his poetry's sharp-edged portrayal of American Indian revolution and realities, or Leo Romero with his wry poems about Celso – the alcohol fueled back-country mystic of the Sangre de Cristo Mountains. Perhaps the finest reading ever at Burnt Horses was the one given by N. Scott Momaday, the Pulitzer

Prize winning author of *House Made of Dawn*. Momaday requested that all of the shop's lights be turned off except for the floor lamp next to a great stuffed armchair, which he possessed with all the authority of his great Kiowa warrior's body. Then, while the audience sat around him like children gathered for story hour, many of us on the floor at his feet, he read in his powerful, resonant voice passages from his novel *The Ancient Child*, complete with separate personae for Billy the Kid and Sitting Bull.

Since I worked in Burnt Horses, I frequently organized the readings and with time grew to be close friends with a number of local writers. For me, the Santa Fe poet whose work shone with a special, transcendent radiance was John Knoll. An heir to both the Surrealists and the Beats, Knoll writes poetry that takes the reader to reality's rim, where the sea recedes into Luis Buñuel's palm, a redwood dreams the world, and Persephone drowns in a heart-shaped pool while a whiskey priest performs her last rites. Living through the 1960's most incendiary days and exploring the psyche's deepest reaches, Knoll labors in unjust obscurity in a small trailer at the edge of the Pojoaque Indian reservation. He is a living saint of the word.

In 1987, John and I began to do readings together when we organized a commemoration at Burnt Horses of the 30th anniversary of Jack Kerouac's *On the Road*. Later, we teamed up with jazz bassist John Clark, and the three of us began doing jazz-poetry improvisations around Santa Fe in various bookstores and venues devoted to experimental theater. These shows drew the attention of Robert Winson – Zen priest, performance poet, and student of San Francisco poetry renaissance figure Philip Whalen. Robert had a poetry show on the newly established Santa Fe community station, and he invited us on the program. So, after a decade, I found myself once more in a radio studio.

When we arrived, the studio's bareness surprised me. There were four unadorned white walls, one of them nearly filled by the control room's large glass panel, a suspended mike, and four chairs – so different from the studio of my college campus station with its rock posters, black and white photos of jazz musicians, campus announcements, and the like. While I figured the studio's severity resulted from its newness, the austere atmosphere increased my nervousness, a nervousness born from a long hiatus from any kind of recording studio. Robert sat behind his glassed-in booth, master of the great bank of switches which ranged before him. We were taping the show rather than doing it live, so while a great reel to reel turned, Knoll and I read our poems to the modal fantasies of John Clark's bass. Now and then, Winson would ask us questions about our work and our collaborative efforts. Later, he mixed the recording into a thirty minute segment, and I heard the broadcast in a friend's living room. Since all my other air time has been live, I've never before or since actually heard my voice emerging from a radio set, an experience both exotic and unnerving.

Soon after my appearance on Winson's show, I left Santa Fe and moved to Colorado's Western Slope, where I have continued over the years to do poetry readings on the community radio stations KVNF in Paonia and KAFM in Grand Junction. Whenever I do a broadcast, the experience always evokes a spiritual sensation as my disembodied voice traverses the ether (as they would have said a century ago) to emerge in a small black box miles away from the studio. In *The Posthuman Dada Guide: Tzara & Lenin Play Chess*, Andrei Codrescu explains that the Paleolithic shaman would climb certain trees or mountaintops from where they would psychically communicate with far distant brother or sister shaman. While Codrescu finds an analogy between the internet and this ancient form of shamanic communication, I would suggest that radio, with its incorporeal voices tearing through space, is a stronger parallel. When Marconi and his colleagues invented radio, they found a way for a message to pierce space at the speed of light, allowing two people to communicate over vast distances nearly instantaneously, like the shaman in their trees, or for millions of people to hear one voice at the same time. Essentially, Hemingway got it right in *For Whom the Bell Tolls* when Pilar compares her occult power to see Robert Jordon's future in his palm to the invisible manifestations of radio waves. Both are invisible yet real. I fear that today, with radio being so commonplace, and its commercial uses so mundane or vitriolic, we tend to forget its powerful and miraculous nature.

≈≈≈

Recently, I crossed the Continental Divide to do a reading on KRFC in Ft. Collins, a city built on the transitional zone between the prairie's western edge and the great wall of the Rocky Mountains. And again, I encountered radio's nearly mystical enchantment. An early winter storm had wrapped Ft. Collins in an icy covering that shone with a strange, inner light from the sun's heavily polarized rays. My wife Brenda and I spent the day of my broadcast exploring the city's coffee houses and bookstores. One coffeehouse, a two-story affair near the Colorado State University campus, was packed with undergraduates talking of Derrida or post-colonial African politics or dark energy and downing lattes at tables with wobbly legs and three different kinds of stools, while the shiny knob-covered espresso machines hissed like tired dragons. All the upstairs tables were full, so we landed in the cold downstairs, where a third of the lights didn't work and the posters for student art shows were ten years out of date. Next, we went downtown to a larger coffeehouse-bookstore, a cooperative that supports the publication of *Matter,* a literary magazine. While this place was also crowded, it was warm, and we managed to find a table in the loft, from where we could survey the book-lined walls. There we sat, drank rich chai tea, and read our respective books – Brenda's *The Gift of Black Folk* by W.E.B. DuBois and my newly purchased *Poetry as Insurgent Art,* wherein Lawrence Ferlinghetti writes, "A true poem can create a divine stillness in the world."

After the coffeehouse, we had supper in a little Thai restaurant and in the growing darkness crossed an intersection to the studios of KRFC, where I sat in a glass booth before a mike suspended by a steel armature. While the soundboard meters twitched like nervous insects, Dona Stein, the host of the poetry show, made a series of public service announcements. Finally, she introduced me to her audience, and then my voice entered the microphone.

"I would like to start with a poem entitled 'Chalice of Bronze, River of Moons.'"

Instantly, the transmitter changed the words into electromagnetic impulses that shot through an antenna and, as James Clerk Maxwell predicted they would nearly 150 years before, raced at the speed of light across the prairie to enter hundreds, maybe thousands, of radios and be transformed again into sound waves by wafer-thin speakers.

And remembering my broadcast inspired imaginings in the dusty attics of my childhood, I smiled once again at the marvel of radio.

Journeywork of the Stars

Something had pulled me up from a deep sleep and out of bed. A noise perhaps – one of the cats skittering down the hall, clutching in her little white fangs her favorite stuffed toy, the one that looks like a skinny brown bear. Maybe the sharp snap of the house settling, or a police siren three blocks away on Orchard Avenue. Who knew? But as I lay in bed, staring up at a room vaguely lit by streetlight sneaking through closed blinds, I felt compelled to dress, go outside, and see what was happening in the 3:00 am night.

My wife slept peacefully, her lovely oval face turned to the blue numbers on the digital alarm clock resting on her nightstand, her breathing quiet and steady. A trio of bright northern stars shone through the high quadrilateral windows just under the bedroom's peak. A block away a dog barked, and beyond, there was the faint, seashell sound of a distant jet.

Quietly, I slipped on a denim shirt and a pair of jeans, wincing when the belt's hook clanked against the buckle. Brenda shifted in her sleep, but didn't awaken.

Leaving the bedroom, I crossed through the blue-walled office and down the narrow hall into the living room with its couch, futon, and entertainment center made from some inexpensive blond wood. At the front door I snapped open the lock and stepped outside.

The street was empty. A row of single-story homes built during the Second World War, and embellished in the 1950's with stoops and narrow pillars and brightly painted fake shutters, lined their way like soldiers to a vanishing point several blocks away. Scattered cars were parked along the street, illuminated by blue-white streetlamps. Down the block, in front of a white clapboard house, a white semi-truck loomed like some massive beast escaped from a machine devoured parallel world. Diagonally across the street stood our neighborhood's eccentric barn-shaped house with its old-west wagon wheels, flower-painted wheel barrow, and enormous Christmas wreath that hung over the front picture window no matter the season. In the next house down, a partly drawn curtain revealed the flickering blue glow from an insomniac's TV set. None of this would explain my being roused from bed.

Then I looked up.

Beyond the streetlamps, partly obscured by my neighbor's massive cottonwood tree, a new constellation hung in the sky. I felt a cold snake run up my spine. I've studied the night skies nearly my entire life, and I know them almost better than my own face. How could there be an entirely new set of stars? A single star maybe, resulting from a nova flaring up in the depths of space. But a complete, never before seen constellation? Impossible. Half obscured by cottonwood leaves, the stellar grouping appeared to be an oval cluster of azure stars, rather like the Pleiades seen through a low-powered telescope.

Wanting a clearer view, I sprinted down the street, looking for a spot without trees. My excitement grew as I glanced at the sky every few steps. The day's summer heat was gone, and the air possessed an early morning desert chill. Cicadas and crickets droned in the grassy lawns. The moan of a diesel engine drifted from the train yards a half a mile away, followed by the metallic thunder of shunting freight cars. Closer by, on U.S. 6, a tractor-trailer shifted gears.

After half a block, I reached a space where there were no tree branches or streetlights blocking my view of the sky. There, about three quarters of the way up from the eastern horizon, hovered a new gathering of stars. It was an insupportable apparition, a paradoxical bee-swarm of interstellar lanterns. Like wisps of luminous clouds, tendrils of blue-tinged nebulae pervaded these strange stars, giving me a possible explanation. These were stars that had just been ignited in a contracting cloud of dust and gas that hovered in our galactic neighborhood, perhaps a dozen light years from our solar system. Still, it seemed extremely odd that there had been nothing in the media about these new born stars.

As I peered upwards, my excitement turned to fear. The stars were beginning to move, turning and shifting about each other in a stately dance that grew faster and faster until they spun about like hummingbirds ablaze with anger. This was truly inconceivable. With a shout, I fled up the street towards my home, filled with confused emotions that gyrated between wonder and dread. I must wake up the others and warn them, I thought in a panic.

And then I truly awoke.

I was lying in bed, and everything was the same as it had been at the start of my dream. Brenda was sleeping, her face towards the bedside clock. In the next room, Lucy, our black cat, was playing with some toy across the hardwood floor. Through the open window, I could hear the thrumming of a train diesel gaining speed, followed by the wounded-beast call of its horn. A few stars even shone through the bedroom's high northern widows, probably some of the brighter suns in Ursa Major, the Great Bear.

As my dream terror subsided, I knew there was no need to leave the safe cocoon of our bed and run outside. Of course, a new constellation did not blaze in the sky. Rather, it dwelled in my unconscious, one of two reoccurring dreams of a celestial nature that have haunted my nights since I was in my teens. The other also involves a fantastic sky object, a planet about half the size of a full moon and colored a luminous shade of turquoise. In that dream, there is no fear, only wonder as I watch it rise from the darkly forested hills of my boyhood home in upstate New York.

Carl Jung would say these objects in the heavens represent my true nature, what he called the Self. The new star cluster is a psychic mandala set in motion, the turquoise planet a representation of my innermost archetypal identity. In support of this interpretation, these dreams often emerge when major shifts are about to happen in my life, or I need to make important decisions. Regardless of whether my Jungian interpretations of these dreams are correct, I do know they are rooted in my lifelong fascination for the cosmos.

≈≈≈

When I was thirteen, my parents bought me my first telescope. It was a three-inch Newtonian reflector with a diminutive spotter scope bolted to the side. A Newtonian reflector draws light into a long steel tube, its interior painted a dull black. At the tube's base, a large concave mirror reflects the light back to a small diagonal mirror which sends the now focused light to a lens at the telescope's side. The diameter of the main mirror is the size of the scope.

My parents purchased my three-inch Newtonian from a local upstate New York craftsman who had constructed several large telescopes for various universities, including Cornell. I loved his workshop, a high-ceilinged barn-sized structure filled with lenses, mirrors, steel tubes, lathes, sheet-metal cutters, white acetylene tanks for welding, and racks of screwdrivers, wrenches, and rub-ber-headed hammers. The scent of hot solder and steel filings filled the air.

A year later, after I had demonstrated that my passion for the instrument was not just a childish whim, we returned to this wondrous workshop and my parents traded in the three-inch for a four-and-a-quarter inch Newtonian with a pale blue exterior, a black tripod, an array of lenses, and a solar filter. I have this scope to this day, almost five decades later.

Once I had the four-and-a-quarter inch telescope in my possession, I be-came obsessed with studying the night skies. Summer was the best season to do this. With school out and the nights warm, I could stay up well past midnight gazing at the great wheel of constellations overhead. After these summertime tele-scopic explorations, I would sit in my stuffy upstairs bedroom, the front window wide open, and the fan turned full speed like the propeller of a P-40 Warhawk flying into battle, while the cicadas and the crickets sang in the dark beyond the window screen. At my desk, under the lonely blue light of a fluorescent lamp, I would pour over the star maps found in *The Telescope Handbook and Star Atlas* by Neale E. Howard, the ones with the transparent overlays of deep space objects rendered in blue ink – pond-shaped splats for nebulae, dotted circles for star clus-ters, and disks for galaxies. The very existence of these exotic interstellar objects stirred my imagination, and the Greek and Arabic names of the stars lent the text a mystical air, as if Neale Howard's book were a centuries old alchemical tome from lost Byzantium.

In addition to the amiably warm evenings, the position of the upstate New York night sky in relation to the galaxy also made those summer nights delightful. Our solar system swims near the galaxy's edge, and the Northern Hemisphere's summer night sky faces inward, towards the mysterious galactic center where the stars are the thickest. Therefore, a dragon's horde of stars grace the balmy July skies of New York, and within this stellar cornucopia my favorite regions to study were the constellations Scorpio and Cygnus.

At 42 degrees north latitude, Scorpio rides low along the southern horizon, barely clearing the tree covered hills. Starting from the middle of Scorpio's arc-shaped head – built around the stars Lesath, Elacrab, and Dschubba – a string of bright suns, including the orange-red gem of Antares, curves gracefully down and then back up to form a triangular stinger. Between this stinger and teapot-shaped Sagittarius's spout lies the center of the galaxy, hidden from view by the densest patch of the Milky Way.

Imagine, if you will, that it is a cloudy, late June upstate New York evening, and you are standing at the edge of a hayfield filled with fireflies. When you look towards the firefly swarm's center, the insects appear to be a teeming mass of flashing, darting lights that nearly fill the space just over the field. However, if you look straight up, you will see a mere dozen phosphorescent insects set against a vast darkness. This is essentially how it is when we look at the night sky. What we see as the Milky Way's luminous mist is actually our edgewise view into the galactic lens, the crowded space where the stars are so thick they merge into a glowing river the ancients believed was milk from Hera's breasts.

For the amateur astronomer, the Milky Way is a phantasmagoria of deep space objects and myriad crystalline stars strewn across the sky. On those July nights decades ago, I would point the telescope in the direction of the galactic center, and delight in the Milky Way's radiant cloud as it resolved into thousands of stars. I would also study in Scorpio's stinger the open star clusters M6 and M7 – brilliant blue-white stellar aggregates mixed with clouds of gas and dust called nebulae, where infant stars are born. Then, in neighboring Sagittarius, I would turn the scope to M22, a globular cluster. Made up from many thousands of reddish-yellow stars that were already old when our sun was born, globular clusters are remnants from the galaxy's youth. Hovering outside the galactic lens, these spherical collections of suns appear to be tiny phosphorescent puffballs that have wandered off from the great stream of the Milky Way.

Although it also dwells in the Milky Way, Cygnus the Swan is a very different constellation from Scorpio. Whereas Scorpio is made up mostly from elderly red and yellow suns sidling along the horizon, the great cross shape of Cygnus flies directly overhead, its young suns blazing whitely with vigorous thermonuclear fires. Indeed, Deneb, the brightest star in Cygnus, is one of the galaxy's biggest and most energetic suns, and at 1500 light years away, the furthest individual star we can discern with the naked eye. Being within the galactic lens, Cygnus, like Scorpio, provides many places where one can resolve the Milky Way's glowing clouds into vast numbers of individual stars. However, at the swan's tail, where Deneb dwells, the Milky Way splits into two streams, a scar called the Great Rift that cuts across heaven's bright tributary. Recent anthropological discoveries indicate that the native peoples who built the Hopewell Indian Mounds viewed the Milky Way as a stream of souls rising from the earth towards an afterlife. For these ancient dwellers of the Ohio River basin, the Great Rift was the gateway to this other world, and Deneb, standing at the head of this dark opening, was the judge of the dead, equivalent to the Egyptian god Osiris.

The summer, with its warm nights and rich viewing field of the galactic lens, has remained my favorite season to study the night sky. However, in my early days as an amateur astronomer, the other seasons received a nearly equal share of my nighttime attention. Throughout the year, the planets ride the ecliptic, and on many autumn evenings sharp with frost or vernal nights damp from the thawing earth, I would study the children of the sun through my Newtonian reflector – the merest dot of light that is Mercury, the dazzling crescent of Venus, the white-capped rusty disk of Mars, the banded orb of Jupiter with its pinprick moons, and dusty yellow Saturn with its mysterious rings. (Uranus and Neptune are so distant that in a telescope the size of mine they are essentially indistinguishable from stars, and very dim ones at that.)

Of course, the Moon also frequents the night skies throughout all four seasons. Since I did not own a lunar filter, any manifestation of the moon past quarter phase was too bright for study, hurting my eyes and leaving dark, unnerving afterimages. However, I often examined the crescent moon, its craters and mountains sharply etched by pure black shadows in the lunar dawn.

The most extreme viewing I did as a young astronomer took place in winter. In upstate New York, the winter nights often drop into the teens, and sometimes reach below zero. But there are some amazing deep space objects that would pull me out into the frigid darkness, including the Pleiades' fiery gems, the Beehive open star cluster in Gemini, and most especially the blue-white wings of the Orion Nebula, its young stars blazing like newly ignited phosphorous. One especially icy night, while observing the Orion Nebula, my eyelid froze to the steel-sheathed eyepiece, and I had to rub the lens with my finger to warm it up enough to peel my eyelid off without tearing any skin. After that, I was more cautious about observing on nights that went below 20 degrees.

≈≈≈

Once I started college, my astronomical activities began to wane. Still, they have remained an important part of my life. Over the decades, I have continued to bring the telescope out when the evenings are clear and the spirit moves me, especially when something special is happening in the sky.

Occasionally there are lunar eclipses, produced when the earth's shadow swallows the moon, turning it into a blood-red orb that casts a fabulous and eerie glow. Then there are the ominous days when the moon eclipses the sun, and though I've never seen a full eclipse, I have watched many partials, studying them through my telescope's solar filter as the moon's perfect black circle slides silently across the sun's disk, slowly devouring the ash-grey sunspots one by one, like some vast cosmic snake. When I would return to upstate New York, I might see the silent, ghostly pulsing of the Aurora Borealis, the Northern Lights. One late autumn night, the aurora engulfed the entire sky with shimmering white curtains. Near midnight, these curtains transformed into an enormous dove that flexed its wings before dissolving into the iridescent zenith. During the years I lived in the Alleghany Mountains of Virginia, there were star parties hosted by my friend and fellow English professor Herb West, a tall angular man with a full beard and a fine laugh. Herb would set up his six-inch reflecting telescope on his home's back deck under the tulip trees, and we would study deep space objects while giant Luna moths settled on the glass doors, drawn by the faint yellow lamplight inside. It was from Herb's house that I saw Halley's Comet on a cold March evening in 1986.

Later that year I moved to New Mexico, where I would begin to dwell under the remarkably clear skies across the arid West.

My introduction to the high desert night was during my first journey west three years before moving to Santa Fe. It was near midnight, and I was crossing Idaho on U.S. 20, when somewhere between Carey and Mountain Home I began glancing out my side window up at the sky. I could see even from the speeding pick-up that the stars were out and looking very promising, so I pulled to a stop on the shoulder, snapped off the headlights, stepped out, and caught my breath in amazement.

The night sky was flawless and filled with suns.

In my whole life I had never seen a sky so amazing. Unobstructed by moisture or city lights, the stars shone with a splendid intensity in the desert air. I stood transfixed, staring up at those clean, cold lights in their uncounted thousands. The only part of the sky that was obscured was far to the south where an impossibly distant thunderstorm produced silent pulses of light that outlined the distant volcanic hills. This was the ideal night sky I had always wished to see.

Three other celestial encounters under western skies especially stand out for me.

One was Comet Hyakutake, which I saw one March night in 1996 while driving south of Ridgway, a village in western Colorado. In an echo to my Idaho experience, I spotted the comet through my truck window, and pulled over to study it. It hung suspended in the northwestern skies over the Ridgway Reservoir, misty white and mysterious, it's head and tail distinct and altogether about the size of the moon. There was something strange about seeing it hovering over the flat, darkened waters, which reflected the brightest stars and the occasional red flash of a buoy light but not the comet, which seemed illusory as it floated above the stone ramparts of Log Hill Mesa. But Hyakutake, which passed a mere 9.3 million miles from the earth, closer than any comet in 200 years, was certainly no illusion.

The second western sky object of note was another comet, but this one was quite unique, a far different sight than Comet Hyakutake.

I first spotted Comet Holmes on All Saints Day, 2007. In binoculars it resolved into a fuzzy white sphere with a bright, pinhead core. The next night, I trained my telescope on it. The comet filled the field, odd and unsettling, a ball of light with a brighter spot in the center, the comet's nucleus. This comet was especially exotic because, while it was larger in the night sky than the moon, it had no tail.

The third night, I simply observed it with the naked eye. It was blue-white dot with a barely visible mist around it, like a star surrounded by a nebula. I was impressed by how far it had moved through the constellation of Perseus. Only the moon, the inner planets, and comets move that quickly against the night's fixed background of stars.

Later, I read that Comet Holmes, journeying out from the sun, had begun to rapidly expand and disintegrate as it reached the region of the solar system between Mars and Jupiter. This was why it had leapt from a +17 magnitude object, so dim it could only be seen through a telescope, to a magnitude of +2, ranking it amongst the second tier of brightest stars. A number of ideas circulated concerning the comet's spectacular demise, but the leading hypothesis proposed that the sun's heat had formed a crust on the comet, and as the ice beneath that crust turned to gas, it built up pressure until the crust exploded, spewing debris to form a vast illuminated sphere literally larger than the sun.

The third remarkable astronomical event I experienced in the West was the transit of Venus across the Sun, which took place on June 5th, 2012. It will not happen again for over a century.

I was standing on the sidewalk of U.S. 66 in Flagstaff, Arizona on that bright June day, just downhill from the famous Lowell Observatory, where at the turn of the 20th century, Perceval Lowell mapped what he thought were the canals of Mars, and where in 1930, Clyde Tombaugh discovered Pluto. A dozen or so amateur astronomers had set up telescopes in front of Old Town's red brick and stucco businesses. They were welcoming passerby to see this rare demon-stration of planetary motion, and I am most grateful to them, for it was through their generosity that I witnessed the transit of Venus. In one amateur's six-inch scope, I could see the sphere of the sun, big and pale white, with a scattering of small sunspots, each containing the black central umbra, and the lighter grey outer penumbra. And there, a tiny black dot, was Venus, crawling across the Sun like a brave explorer slipping past the gaze of a massive, flame- engorged demon. For me, this was an incredibly moving sight, because that diminutive planetary circle passing across the face of the titanic sun demonstrates our true place in creation. Just like Venus, the Earth is a miniscule sphere spinning around a mighty star which is but one of billions of stars in a galaxy that is journeying through a universe containing billions of galaxies.

And herein lies the inestimable value of astronomy – it reveals humanity's deep interconnection with the universe, as well as our fundamental origins in the cosmos.

Over five billion years ago an ancient red-giant star went supernova, seeding a nearby cloud of dust and gas, a nebula like the one in Orion, with a myriad of elements – carbon, calcium, copper, zinc, silver, and many others – forged during the star's long life of fusing atoms. The supernova also sent shockwaves throughout the nebula, causing it to compress into diffuse spheres that contracted and solidified as they gathered more and more of the dust and gas. At the center of these newly conceived objects, a monstrous sphere consumed great swaths of the nebula, finally becoming massive enough to fuse its hydrogen and helium atoms in a spontaneous burst of nuclear fire. In this titanic ignition, our sun was born. Soon after, smaller spheres, already in orbit around the new star, coalesced into the planets. And as the eons passed on the third planet, the heavier elements, shaped in the heart of the deceased star and strewn into the nebula that cradled our solar system, shaped oceans and continents and finally life – plants, amphibians, reptiles, and mammals. Run your hands across your arms. Feel the contours of your face. You are touching structures formed from atoms generated by a supergiant star that exploded millions of years before the earth even existed. And then travel more deeply in time. All of this – your face, the planets, the sun, the supergiant star which triggered the sun's birth – are a part of the Big Bang, the eruption of the universe from a single point, a fourteen billion year old quantum blast that is still unfolding. As Walt Whitman observed, and I have quoted earlier, "I believe a leaf of grass is no less than the journeywork of the stars."

And so, like a wanderer returning home to visit his old haunts, I still take out the telescope my parents gave me to view the night sky.

I store the scope in the room behind the garage, and when I want to view a celestial object – the moon, or Saturn, or the globular cluster in Hercules – I heft the awkward arrangement of mirrors and steel tubes, and carry it past the washing machine and drier, the black tripod banging against their white metal sides. Once past the rear door, I find a spot in the backyard where the house's shadow blocks the streetlights, and I also have a clear view of the ecliptic. Next, I return to the garage room, picking up the palm-sized white box that holds the eyepieces – small black cylinders with lenses in their dark chambers, encircled in bubble wrap like jewels of steel and glass.

Usually I start with a low-power lens with a wide field of view and slide it into the stainless-steel tube high on the scope's side. The desert night air is cool but not cold, for it is mid-August, near midnight. The sounds of crickets and a car sliding by on a far-off street accompany my observing. Scorpio and Sagittarius are a bit too low for good viewing, but Cygnus is approaching the zenith, so I swing the scope up and aim it for the densest patch of the Milky Way – the breast-milk of Hera, the Hopewell pathway of souls. Having crossed hundreds of parsecs of space, the light from thousands of stars completes its voyage by racing down the darkly painted interior of the hollow cylinder, striking the four-and-a-quarter inch convex mirror at its terminus, and reflecting back to a perfectly angled two-inch oval mirror resting on a metal plate held to the scope's walls by a slender metal rod. From the oval mirror, the light passes through the eyepiece and, magnified, enters my eye and strikes my synapses. A drift of glowing mist becomes a tight spray of blue-white points, the confirmation that when we look at the Milky Way, we are viewing the densest edge of the galactic lens.

After spending some time exploring Cygnus, I move on to Jupiter, hovering fat and bright in Capricorn. Its bands are colorful and clear this night, and its moons range in a startlingly straight line to either side of its yellow-white disk – one of Galileo's proofs for a heliocentric solar system.

The night's final object is M31, the great spiral galaxy in Andromeda, which has just cleared the neighbor's garage. Looking like an eye-shaped piece of the Milky Way torn and tossed from the Swan's heart, the light from the Andromeda Galaxy, produced by billions of suns, has journeyed nearly two million light years to reach my scope's mirrors.

After returning the telescope and lenses to their dwelling place in the room behind the garage, I retire to the glassed-in back porch, sit down at my desk, and flick on a small, high-intensity lamp. Its sharply defined cone of light illuminates the star charts in Howard's *The Telescope Handbook and Star Atlas*, and I study the black dots of suns on the white background, occasionally placing the transparent overlay with its ovals and circles of galaxies and nebulae. I begin with Cygnus, where I had travelled that night, moving out in circles that eventually take in even the constellations of the Southern Hemisphere – Crux, Sculptor, Piscis Austrinus, Chamaeleon, and others.

As the two a.m. hour approaches, I am content. I close the book, turn off the lamp, and head off to bed. It's not long before I enter the dark realm of sleep, where I find myself running down the street to gaze up at a constellation of strange new stars dancing in late summer sky.

The View from Uncompahgre

Beginning with my childhood in the heart of the Allegany Highlands and continuing into my adult years on the borderlands of the Colorado Plateau, my search for the transcendent – the foundational reality behind the mask of appearances – has resulted in many strange and unexpected experiences. Why I have been on this quest, I cannot say. I seem to have been born with the desire to slide past the world's sharp edges and witness the marvels that live behind the theatrical sets confining our vision. Even today, when I glimpse the deep currents running under the world's surface, I experience the kind of wonder a child feels the first time she uses a prism to translate a stream of pure white light into the spectrum's complex presentation. I am feeling it now as I write these words, for outside my glassed-in study, thousands of cottonwood seeds swirl and tumble like fat snowflakes in the wind, gathering in piles outside my door, a February blizzard miraculously manifested in late May, despite the desert heat.

One of my first encounters with this subterranean reality took place when I was six years old. I was raised in upstate New York, not far from the Pennsylvania border, in a valley carved by retreating glaciers. My father, to supplement his income, planted several acres in blue spruce to sell for landscaping and Christmas trees. The rows of turquoise-tinged evergreens formed the perfect setting for childhood adventures. Wandering through the spruce, I would sometimes crawl past the prickly needles into the tight space under the bottommost branches, where I would smell the moist earth and the fragrant sap that would stick to my hands and bare arms.

Our century old neo-classical home, with its white clapboard siding and square pillars, faced the dirt-surfaced Brown Road. For someone standing on the porch, the driveway was to the right, and along it stood a row of three maples and a locust, some of the tallest trees in the valley. Beyond the trees and the driveway, the blue spruce rows ranged alongside the dirt road and under phone lines suspended from a series of creosote soaked wood poles. On one June afternoon, I was playing in the spruce under those wires. A strong wind blew from the southwest, soughing through the thick needled evergreen branches. This sound was familiar. But on that day I noticed a different set of tones – an eerie, humming mix ranging through various pitches and keys.

Now, months before, John Glenn had made his historical orbital journey, an event I watched with rapt attention on our small black and white vacuum tube television. President Kennedy had recently pledged we would reach the moon by decade's end, and my own father worked in a defense plant building guidance systems for those tiny Mercury capsules hurtling through the void. I religiously watched *The Twilight Zone* and my favorite toy was a space helmet with a green visor. To add to this heady mix, there had been a rash of UFO sightings in the area, so, when I heard those strange singing tones, I naturally concluded they were extraterrestrial in origin.

My father worked second shift, and soon after I heard the strange sound, he emerged from the backdoor to head to work in the family car, a massive Chrysler station wagon with push button transmission. When I called to him, he crossed the short distance from the driveway to where I stood under the phone lines. The wind was gusting, and the wires were humming nicely.

When he asked me what was up, I pointed towards the hazy blue sky, and shouted for him to hear what I was hearing – a flying saucer.

He picked me up, and I was next to his round, smiling face with its neat black mustache. Standing for a time in the warm afternoon sun, he listened to the rattle of the maple leaves, the ocean sound of the spruce in the wind, and, yes, the mysterious singing. Then he laughed and explained that my flying saucer was the wind passing through the wires and making them vibrate.

"Listen. The sound will stop when the wind dies."

I did as he asked, and indeed, the sound faded with the wind.

"All right," he said, and set me down. "I have to go to work."

I watched as he walked back to the station wagon, waved, and climbed in. The engine started, and the blue Chrysler rolled out with a crunch of tires on loose gravel. As he turned onto the dirt road, a cloud of dust enveloped the vehicle, and soon he was out of sight past the woodlot. As the spruce shadows slowly shifted across the grassy ground, I listened to the humming, disappointed at first that it was not produced by an alien craft from another star. Gradually, however, I became fascinated that such a strange and fabulous sound could be generated by something as simple as wind through wire. Though I certainly could not express it, I sensed in that moment the transcendent power of an interconnected universe that could create the blue spruce, the yellow-orange sun, the Chrysler station wagon, and the eerie steel vibration that evoked other planets hovering beyond the bright sky.

Much later I would read, "The Judgment of the Birds." In it, Loren Eiseley, an anthropologist and essayist, encourages us to discover the remarkable experiences hidden in everyday occurrences. He describes a quintet of commonplace moments – a flight of pigeons in a city's pre-dawn light, a crow lost in the fog, a swarm of desert warblers, arboreal birds singing in the face of death, and a spider surviving the autumn's frost in a streetlamp. In each of these, Eiseley finds a miracle. He explains that his essay is intended for readers "who are capable of discerning in the flow of ordinary events the point at which the mundane world gives way to quite another dimension."

Though I did not know it cognitively at the age of six, this is what I intuited when my father explained the sound of the wires in the wind.

≈≈≈

Over the years, I would encounter more of these instances of the transcendent, sometimes in surprising settings.

When I was a junior in college, I landed a summer job at the same factory where my father helped build guidance systems. My task was certainly not as skilled as his. Working third shift, I operated the acid bath that etched copper plates for circuit boards. Occasionally, during my lunch hour, instead of finding a quiet corner of the break room to read a novel, I would wander the plant. It was a fascinating place at three a.m. Empty, fluorescent-lit corridors led to vast chambers sitting in near-darkness, their elaborate machinery covered in shadows. Some nights, I would chance on a hallway window with its blinds up, revealing an expansive room holding rows of lit desks where quiet workers toiled at mysterious tasks, some with oscilloscopes and magnetometers, others with documents and typewriters.

On one of these excursions, I entered a maze of corridors I had never taken. Most of the doors I passed had combination locks, their compartments either totally dark or concealed behind windowless walls. After a number of these sealed sections, I came upon a short series of large plate glass windows behind which stretched a brightly lit chamber filled with rank upon rank of tall white and grey computers. This was a decade before the digital revolution and these were old-style main frame computers with magnetic tape running between big aluminum reels that would suddenly start up, spin for a time, and then abruptly stop. But even more bizarre, at the edge of these rows of computers, a man in a white shirt, black pants, and neat black tie sat on a wooden stool, hand to chin, staring at the machines immediately in front of him. He was thin, totally bald, and wore heavy black-frame glasses.

I stood at the window for maybe fifteen minutes, transfixed by this figure peering at his electronic menagerie, the high priest of a cavernous temple filled with shining altars to the gods of technology. Uneasy, I kept expecting him to glance up and see me, but he never did. As the minutes passed, the absolute strangeness of the scene built up a nervous charge. It was three a.m., the hour of surreal dreams and sorcery, and here was this motionless man in the secret heart of a technological Delphi. It was as if I my presence were taboo. Abruptly I left, and never again returned to that place.

≈≈≈

After completing my university training, I moved to western Virginia where I lived in a wood clapboard house. Built before the Civil War, it had a double-level front porch, four bedrooms, and a grand living room with a mahogany framed mirror and fireplace. However, it was quite run down, which was why I could afford to rent it. Indeed, only the first floor bedroom, kitchen, bathroom, and sitting room were in use – all heated by a single woodstove. The rest of the rooms were closed off.

Situated on a dirt road that petered out in a dense forest of ash and hickory, the house was surrounded by the wild, Blue Ridge Mountain landscape. The abundant Virginia forestland – with its flowering rhododendrons, tulip trees, red-buds, and wild apples – formed a botanical climax to the upstate New York flora I grew up with. In the summer, I would wade barefoot up the stream that flowed behind the house. Scrub willows, dogwoods, and mulberry trees created a tight canopy of green, filtering the sunlight and softening the colors of the cardinal flowers and daisies covering the banks. Swallowtail butterflies would drift beside me. It was an emerald realm, beyond sin and time. The Edenic atmosphere was increased by two enormous blacksnakes that lived in the top story of a shed behind the house. At times, I would watch them gliding down the ladder from their man-made lair or see them draped from the front yard's hickory tree, like old hoses hanging from a peg.

And yet this fabulous Eden served as a mere backdrop to my most transcendent experience in Virginia. That moment belonged to the fireflies.

≈≈≈

I've always loved fireflies. As a child in upstate New York, I would run into the dark hay fields on moonless June nights as if entering a living galaxy. Thousands of fireflies would blink and swirl and drift on the air's dark currents – a shifting echo of the stars above. We would sometimes chase them with Mason jars, and after capturing two or three dozen, we'd take them to a lightless room and watch them flash within the glass cylinder, emitting a ghostly green light.

There were many nights when I witnessed fireflies in Virginia, but there was only one that surpassed anything from my childhood, becoming a true opening to Eiseley's other dimension. On that particularly warm spring evening, I ate a solitary supper and spent several hours reading in the armchair next to the unlit woodstove. Around 10:30 I grew sleepy, but before going to bed, I decided to head outside first and smell the night air and look at the stars.

Walking down the short foyer, I opened the front door, passed through the porch, and gasped.

There, across the fields and hillsides, streamed tens of thousands of fireflies forming glowing rivers and pools in the Appalachian night. Never had I seen so many fireflies. I dashed back inside to turn off all the lamps so there would be no competition with the insect phosphorescence. Back on the porch steps, I sat down and drank in the spectacle. The waning moon had not yet risen, and in the almost total darkness the fireflies were in full glory – blinking and flashing and flying about, sometimes in random, chaotic firings, sometimes in coordinated patterns, great patches of light turning on and off in complex rhythms.

I sat on those porch steps well past midnight, until exhaustion led me to bed where I dreamed of vast galaxies spinning and merging in the void.

≈≈≈

Not long after this grand night of the fireflies, I moved to the American Southwest where I began to explore numerous ancient American Indian sites, especially the great ruined cities of the Anasazi and the sacred art carved or painted on boulders and cliffs by desert tribes stretching back five thousand years. The power of these places derives in part from their evocation of time. Many Indian peoples, from the deepest past to the present, possess a fundamental understanding of time – its rhythms, its causes, and its role in determining the cycles of the hunt, the planting and harvesting of crops, and the journey of the soul. Time is intricately connected with American Indian mythology, and the Maya even envisioned days, months, and years as gods.

One recent summer, I was struck by the transcendent power of this connection after three encounters with sacred time on Indian ground.

The first took place at Aztalan, a northern community of the Cahokian people. Stretching from Wisconsin to the lower Mississippi River basin, the Cahokian civilization flourished from 700 to 1400 C.E., influencing American Indian culture and society from the Midwestern prairies to the Atlantic coast. According to Robert A. Birmingham and Lynne G. Goldstein in their book *Aztalan*, contemporary tribes that continue to adhere to Cahokian mythology, ritual, and social organization include the Natchez, Choctaw, Chickasaw, Creek, and Cherokee.

The political and religious capital of this civilization was Cahokia, a Pre-Columbian city covering five square miles located near East St. Louis. At its height in 1150 C.E., Cahokia held 20,000 people, over a thousand thatch homes, and 120 pyramidal mounds of varying sizes constructed from stone and earth. A two-mile-long stockade protected the city's central district with its temples, palaces, and grand plazas. Cahokia was also the site of Woodhenge, a circle of 20-foot-high posts nearly 500 feet in diameter used by priests as a solar calendar. However, the city's gem is Monk's Mound, its four terraces rising 100 feet from its base. Covering more ground than the Great Pyramid at Giza, Monk's Mound is the largest earthen structure in North America, and once held the homes of Cahokia's mightiest lords and priests.

While far smaller than Cahokia, Aztalan, at 500 inhabitants, was still one of the largest Cahokian settlements. It consisted of three major platform mounds, 80 smaller mounds, and a log and plaster palisade 20 feet high that surrounded the entire complex. The largest mound was a two-step pyramid rising 16 feet and covering 8,000 square yards. Like Monk's Mound at Cahokia, it held the dwelling of the "brothers of the sun" – the rulers and chief priests who were responsible for keeping a balance between the orderly gods of the sky and the dark spirit beings of the chaotic underworld. At 350 miles from Cahokia, Aztalan was the northernmost outpost of the Cahokian realm, and thus a place vital to both trade and defense.

When I settled in the Southwest, I became interested in Cahokia because
of my fascination for Chaco Canyon, a complex of twelve multi-storied stone
and plaster "great houses" that rested on the Colorado Plateau's southeastern
edge. At 10,000 people, Chaco Canyon was the heart of the Anasazi civilization,
and the two cultures, comparable in size and achievement, were both at their
height in the 12th century C.E. It is likely that they shared trading routes, and
perhaps philosophical and theological concepts as well. As late as 1542, when the
Pecos Indians of New Mexico told the Spanish conquistador Francisco Vasquez
de Coronado that off in the distant prairie to the east there stood a vast city of
gold and turquoise ruled by a mighty emperor, they were probably referring to
the abandoned Cahokia. So, when my wife Brenda and I travelled to Madison,
Wisconsin to visit her sister, I took advantage of the trip to visit Aztalan, my first
encounter with a Cahokian site.

On a hot June day we left Madison, and after a thirty minute drive on a
country highway through gently rolling fields of wheat, corn, and hay, we reached
the periphery of Aztalan State Park. At the parking lot, a scattering of small
mounds stood guard, and I climbed one. Later, I would read that the people of
Aztalan erected poles in these mounds for their Green Corn Ceremony, which
celebrated the sprouting of new crops in high summer. About twelve feet high
and covered in thick grass, the mound gave me a view of the reconstructed stockade. A wall of twenty foot high logs extending hundreds of feet, the stockade
had once formed a sizable protective structure, rectangular in shape, enclosing
the Cahokian settlement. There was a large break in the wall's two sections, and
through it I could make out the much larger Northwest Platform Mound, where
the elite of Aztalan buried their dead.

With great anticipation, I left the small mound and Brenda lead the way
down a path through the site's calf high grasses. Soon we were traversing along
the wall, feeling dwarfed by its protective bulk. Passing the Northwest Platform
Mound, we followed the wooden rampart until we reached the Main Platform
Mound – a massive, two-tiered earthen pyramid that had been the home of the
city's chieftains. Climbing its grassy sides, we reached the pyramid's apex and
faced towards the unseen Crawfish River, Aztalan's western border.

Brenda's slender form was still and centered, her right hand shading her
short blond hair and blue eyes as she gazed across the ruined city. To the north,
east, and south, the stockade wall formed three sides of a sizable rectangle. To the
west, the stockade was largely unreconstructed, and so the view was open to a
forest of oaks, maples, and ash dense with heavy grey trunks and full green leaves.

Between us and the forest, a low, round glacial knoll stood in the humid air. Overhead, the sun, hot and white, demanded a sacrifice. My thoughts dropped back nearly a thousand years. Aztalan's expanse became filled with men, women, and children in plant-fiber shawls, chanting to the drums' steady rhythm. Beyond them, aisles of square, thatch-roofed dwellings occupy the urban space within the high walls. The smokes of scattered cooking fires bisect the blazing sky, turkeys wander the avenues, and fields of young corn flash in the sunlight as the wind ripples across the city. On the pyramid, a priest in purple and red robes decorated with shells and copper beads emerges from the wood-sided palace. He stands before an elaborately carved altar, burns copal brought up from the lands of the stone pyramids far to the south, and sings prayers to a life-giving sun pulsing with light and heat.

Later, as we drove back to Madison, Brenda noted that it was the solstice – the longest day of the year, the beginning of summer. I was delighted. In the drift of travelling, I had lost track of the calendar, and there was something magic about ascending the central pyramid of Aztalan on the solstice without being aware of the date, as if some centuries-old ceremony had drawn us to witness the sun at zenith in that sacred place. As I watched the green fields of corn and hay roll past, I knew I had certainly encountered the transcendent in that lost outpost of an ancient culture.

≈≈≈

My second encounter that summer with American Indian sacred time took place nearly two months later and 1500 miles away. One of the most important petroglyph sites in the American Southwest, Utah's Parowan Gap is a deep, V shaped cut or pass in a volcanic ridge that separates the Great Basin Desert from the mountainous western reaches of the Colorado Plateau. This cut is perfectly aligned so that its eastern opening directly faces the rising sun on the Summer Solstice, and its western opening the setting sun on the Winter Solstice.

A millennia ago, the Fremont Indians, named for the explorer who discovered their artifacts, used Parowan Gap as an observatory, recording the cyclic patterns of the sun, moon, and Venus in hundreds of petroglyphs carved in the stone faces throughout the cut. Essentially, Parowan Gap was the 11th century equivalent to the banks of computers I encountered in my three a.m. wanderings at the upstate New York defense plant. The Fremont, who created this visual data bank of astronomical and mythological data, were contemporaries with the Great House Anasazi of Chaco Canyon and the pyramid builders of Cahokia. However, being more dependent on hunting, the Fremont dwelled in humble villages of brush houses or single-story stone structures, directing their potential architectural energies into religious ceremony and extensive petroglyph sites like those at Parowan Gap.

One mid-August morning, my teenage daughters and I approached Parowan Gap from the west off of Utah Route 130. It was our second visit to the site. We arrived just before dawn to avoid the sun's heat, and the volcanic ridge loomed long and dark against the pale blue horizon. Upon reaching the ridge I slowed, sliding the car gently through the gap's great stone ramparts.

At the far end we pulled into a small dirt parking lot. As we got out, I grabbed a small black daypack that held a guidebook and three steel water bottles that clanked dully in the holy silence.

Just then the sun cleared the low volcanic hills, and the dawn's coolness fled into the shadows. A yellow blaze illuminated Parowan Gap's centerpiece. Named the V-Gap Calendar Petroglyph, this ten-foot high panel contains many figures – suns, moons, shaman, birds, snakes, footprints, rows of circles arranged within rectangles, and a star-shaped glyph anthropologists believe represents Venus. The centerpiece of this ensemble is a great V that ends in a rounded shape like the bottom of an alchemist's flask. There are 182 notches on this V, the number of sunsets between the winter and summer solstice.

Following the left line of the V, one sees high on the brown volcanic rockface one of the gap's most fascinating petroglyphs. Next to a ghost-like torso of a shaman, the Fremont carved a large circle with three circles hanging from it – the middle one straight down and the other two at 45 degree angles. Within these circles are smaller, concentric circles. The whole figure looks remarkably like the age-old symbol for a pawn shop. But its real meaning involves the solar year. The large circle represents the sun. The smaller circle directly underneath represents both the vernal and autumnal equinoxes, the circle to the left the winter solstice, and the circle to the right the summer solstice. Thus the figure depicts the movement of the sun from solstice to solstice, like the golden disc at the end of a great clock pendulum swinging back and forth.

We studied the panel until the growing heat sent us into the gap. It felt like we were descending into the earth as its steep, rocky slopes loomed above us, and the air was noticeably cooler. But the sun was gaining ground, devouring the shadows. Blond and fair-skinned, my daughters, Ursula and Isadora, kept out of the sun as much as possible. As we made our way between the road and the south-facing slope, we spotted many stone carvings – spirals, a segmented snake with horns, a fan of lines, parallel waves of dots, an owl's wing, bird tracks, a spider web, and many more. All of it had to do with celestial cycles and their relationship to spirituality, ritualism, hunting, and agriculture – a vast temple to humanity's place in the cosmos.

When we reached a panel depicting a bat hovering over a crescent moon and spiral, we decided to cross the road. On our previous visit the year before, we hadn't spent much time on the north-facing side of the gap, and so we wanted to focus on its, for us, largely unseen carvings.

Seeking the petroglyphs higher up, we found a trail that lead to an uneven ledge atop a mound built from the cliff's rubble. With my daughters following, I carefully made my way over crumbling stones past abstract grids of lines and arcs, a spiral, and tall hash-marked cylinders that looked like ancient plants from the Triassic.

After about fifteen minutes, we arrived at a set of unique images on a large vertical stone face. At eye level we saw a flower shape, much like an orchid, with a small oval center. From this center, two lines curve down like a long tail or a meandering stream. Two dotted lines start from opposite sides on the bottom of the flower. These lines arc out and then flow with the tail, which ends about two feet from where the cliff face had fractured, leaving a sharp, lower edge and a block-shaped gap. From this edge, an inverted teardrop shape, encompassing a set of horizontal lines, arises. To the teardrop's right, a carved corn stalk with three sets of paired leaves rests in the stone. The sun, which had just cleared the north side of the cut, shone directly on this particular stone slab, and its carved forms were fully lit.

My daughters and I crouched on the low cliff mound, studying these mysterious petroglyphs while the solar light shifted on the rock face. Finally, Isadora spoke up, her voice sounding like a high-pitched flute's in the sun-drenched air.

"I wonder what these mean?"

"I'm not sure," I answered. "Let's see what the book says."

Sliding the daypack off my shoulders, I pulled out the guidebook – *The Parowan Gap: Nature's Perfect Observatory*, V. Garth Norman's report on the 2002 Parowan Gap Archeological Project. I poked around in it until I found the sketch of our cliff face. As I read the anthropologists' interpretation of these petroglyphs – an interpretation based both on archeological studies and on information provided by the modern descendants of the Fremont Indians – I felt an eerie, light-headed sensation, like a child's reaction to an "extraterrestrial" encounter with wind-humming phone wires.

A thousand years ago, an artist created a set of images to portray the inter-connection between his people's planting mythology and the cycles of the sun. His body had long since turned to dust, but his carvings in stone still functioned perfectly.

In *The Parowan Gap*, Norman explains that there are twelve lines in the inverted teardrop shape that balloons up from the rock face's edge. He identifies this teardrop as a cocoon. Above it, what my daughters and I thought was a flower, is actually a butterfly hatching from the cocoon, and the corn stalk is a corn-deity who is half-human, half-plant. With its twelve lines, the cocoon is a calendar, and what it marks are the beginning and ending of the all-important 105-day vegetation cycle. The first day of the cycle signals when to plant, and the last day when to harvest. The butterfly's metamorphosis, Norman explains, represents the emergence of life from the earth, and the corn-deity illustrates the link between human and vegetative fertility.

But, what made me feel a tingling in my spine, like a snake rising up my back, were the dates for the beginning and ending of the 105-day cycle – April 29th and August 12th. These are "the only days in the year when this figure is fully illuminated at sunrise," Norman writes.

And the cocoon, the moth, and the corn-deity were indeed fully illumi-nated by the rising sun, for the day was August 12th. Once again, as had hap-pened on the solstice at Aztalan, I had arrived at a site sacred to the American Indians on a date with major cultural and spiritual significance. Carl Jung would have regarded these moments as prime examples of synchronicity – his term for meaningful coincidences arranged by the collective unconscious. In this light, as I regard my calendrical encounters at Aztalan and Parowan Gap, I believe they confirmed time's elemental connection with the human psyche.

≈≈≈

However, when I had my third and final encounter with sacred time that season, I was fully aware of the significance of the date, and I deliberately chose the place to have my chronometric encounter.

In September, when that summer had nearly run its course, I learned that a relatively rare occurrence was about to take place – the full moon would rise on the autumnal equinox. When the moon is full, it rises at exactly the same time as the sun sets, always a fascinating event to witness. However, since the moon would be full on the equinox, there was an added wonder. On the two equinoxes, day and night are equal, and so with the moon being full, the sun and the moon would be in the sky for an equal amount of time. It would be a magical moment in celestial mechanics, a natural completion to my summer's encounters with sacred time.

About an hour before sunset on September 22nd, my daughters and I left our house and set out across the century-old elm-lined streets of the western Colorado city of Grand Junction.

At the city's southern edge, we turned on Little Park Road, a blacktop highway that winds its way up desert foothills covered in prickly-pear cactus, juniper trees and sparsely clustered stucco houses. Within a dozen minutes we were ascending the north rim of the Uncompahgre Plateau, a vast upland that stretches a hundred miles along its north-south axis – a place of canyons, streams, and great forests of pine, spruce, and aspen.

As far back as ten thousand years ago, tribal peoples flourished on its slopes and rolling tableland summits. Semi-nomadic, they made their way to the canyon depths in winter and the highlands in summer, feasting on abundant game, wild grains, and piñon nuts. Much later, around 1000 C.E., when the Fremont carved the petroglyphs at Parowan Gap and the Cahokians built the pyramid mounds at Aztalan, the Indians of the Uncompahgre Plateau constructed stone towers and circles, the purpose of which remain a mystery. During Spanish colonial times, the Utes occupied the plateau, and in 1761 they served as guides to an explorer named Juan Maria de Rivera, who was the first European to see the confluence of the Colorado and Gunnison rivers, where Grand Junction stands today. A century later, Anglo-Americans, who had replaced the Spanish colonists, forced the Utes off their beloved Uncompahgre Plateau in the last Indian removal of the 19th century. So the ground on which we would view the rising of the equinox moon was definitely sacred, though its loss by the Utes had stained its hallow nature.

After the final twists and turns through high banks of jumbled boulders, we pulled into a small dirt parking area that the BLM had set up for a popular trail. Leaving the car, my daughters and I headed for a collection of rectangular sandstone slabs. Perched atop one, we had an excellent view of the sky's hemisphere. To the south, the land continued to rise in broken sandstone and shale bluffs. To the west stretched a serpentine vastness of canyons and gulches carved in red and beige rock, much of it covered in piñon and juniper. The deepest, Echo Canyon, held a scattering of cottonwoods and Siberian elms along its sandy bottom. Beyond Echo Canyon, the land rose higher and higher until it reached a smooth bench of chalk-white sandstone ending in a pine covered ridge. To the north, the tightly folded ramparts of the Book Cliffs lead eastward to the frozen wave of Mount Garfield – all of it bathed in the ruby light of the setting sun. Due east loomed the great, dark wedge of the Grand Mesa, bisecting the horizon with its straight-lined basaltic summit. The Utes name it Thunder Mountain, and in the winter, the figure of a mythical thunderbird can be seen outlined in snow on its forested slopes.

And in this place, we waited for the moon.

The sun sank from view. Since we were lower than the horizon formed by the Grand Mesa and the Uncompahgre Plateau, we had to wait. If we had been standing on a flat plain, moonrise and sunset would have been at the same time. Instead, it was as if we were observing the event from the bottom of a vast, shallow bowl.

Peering at the sky, looking for the first stars to appear, I felt restless, and shifted several times on our rock. My daughters began to make silly jokes about characters from Japanese Manga. A few small clouds hovered in the darkening sky. Otherwise, the air was crisp and clear, washed by recent rains. A shadow line gradually engulfed the Grand Mesa. We had entered the earth's twilight zone – the evening's transitional realm. The Book Cliffs ceased glowing. The eastern sky turned violet, then silver, then a blue that was almost black. The air grew cold.

And the moon rose.

First there was a sliver of light, dazzling, like burning phosphorous. Slowly, like a massive white fire balloon, the moon floated up away from the Grand Mesa's ponderous mass – first a quarter, next a half, and finally the entire sphere, which looked for a moment as if it were resting on the mesa's summit. But soon it broke free, climbing the sky – an orb accompanied by the shimmering blaze of Jupiter, rising in tandem further south along the mesa's edge.

Isadora sang a haunting, wordless song, while Ursula and I gazed in silence. Standing on the line between yin and yang, the shadow and light, we dwelled at the interface between an equal day and night, the ephemeral full moon and the ever spherical sun.

It was that summer's final transcendent moment.

~~~

In his documentary *Cave of Forgotten Dreams*, German director Werner Herzog takes the viewer deep into the Cave of Chauvet-Pont-d'Arc, a French site containing some of the oldest cave-paintings in Europe. Created in 34,000 B.C.E., these sacred images are twice as old as those found in the more famous caves of Lascaux and Altamira. On Chauvet's limestone walls, horses and bison parade across the prairie, alongside images of bears, lions, and woolly mammoths.

At the cave's heart, on a hanging stone column, ancient artists painted a wild bull embracing a naked woman's legs and pubis. This is perhaps a depiction of an earth goddess regenerating animals slain in the hunt. Or, it may be the earliest representation of the Minotaur –the offspring of Queen Pasiphaë of Crete and the bull of Poseidon, god of the sea. When the

Greeks acquired this story, they interpreted it negatively, envisioning the Minotaur as a rapacious, flesh-eating monster, and Pasiphaë's act of conception the result of perverse sexual drives brought on by a curse of the gods. For the Bronze Age Greeks were a patriarchal people, whose mythological trend was to view goddess-centered worship as corrupt, binding humankind to the earth. They displaced feminine deities and their focus on sanctified fertility with sky-gods like Zeus and an Aristotelian paradigm that separated the human and natural realms. However, the Chauvet cave paintings return us to the Paleolithic and the original meaning of the Minotaur – that the human and natural spheres intertwine, and a spiritual essence permeates it all. As Werner Herzog explains, the images in Chauvet-Pont-d'Arc affirm that there are no barriers between our world and the mythic world, and that we are not *homo sapiens*, men who know, but are instead *homo spirtualis*, men who are of the spirit.

This vision is innate in the human character. It took us hundreds of thousands of years to attain a scientific understanding of reality. For millennia our explanations for the workings of the universe were mythological – the Great Bear's soul returns to life through a holy dance, the Corn Mother sacrifices herself to give food to a starving people, an invisible Dionysus watches from a massive stone throne as priest-actors perform the *Bacchae*, Quetzalcoatl's penitential journey plunges him into the fiery realm of the dead, Christ's stone burial chamber cracks open on Easter Sunday, the raven on a Himalayan rooftop announces the rebirth of the Dali Lama.

Many people believe that science has robbed us of this mythological vision by denying the existence of the transcendent. I disagree. What science has done is to bring us full circle, back to the animism of the Chauvet cave paintings. Those artists believed that everything – from stars to crickets to limestone caves – possesses spirit, and so existence itself is wondrous and all we need to worship. We have received the same glorious revelation as the ancients. Our sense of awe is again rooted in the universe itself, in the transcendent power of reality. We understand that billions of galaxies fill an inconceivably vast universe, and each galaxy contains a thousand million suns, an inexhaustible grail of time and space, energy and matter. And so like our tribal ancestors, we are once again animists, worshiping the sky and the earth, the sun and the moon, and the faraway stars.

I know this from my encounters with the sublime actualities of the world – telephone wires humming over infant spruce, bright three a.m. computer caverns, fireflies in the Appalachian night, an earthen pyramid under a solstice blaze, calendric petroglyphs on volcanic stone, and the equinox dance of sun and moon.

And therefore, I celebrate the awakened universe – the view from Uncompahgre.

To a Destination Unknown

"In that country time did not exist. There was only the sound of water
hurrying over pebbles to an unknown destination...."
— Loren Eiseley, *The Immense Journey*

I

In western Virginia, there is a house, over a century old, which rests at the base of a grassy hill. When I lived in this house, decades ago, the fields swarmed twice a year with monarchs on their way to and from Mexico, feeding on the abundant wildflowers. Under the butterflies and flowers, at the roots of the grasses, a spring emerged and filled a small stone-lined chamber. An underground pipe carried this water downhill to an open cement cistern in the cellar. This cistern, about the size of an Egyptian sarcophagus, would continually fill with water up to about three inches from its rim, where a short pipe siphoned the water into a circular metal drain. The pipe from the spring rested on the cistern's rim, and the water made a gentle burbling sound as it poured from the pipe and filled the cistern's smooth surfaced pool. When I was depressed or agitated, I would go down to the base-ment, sit in an old cane-bottom chair, and listen to the water, letting it comfort me. It was always cool down there, even on the hottest summer afternoon, and the silvery light that filtered in through the small dusty windows at the top of the cellar walls created the glow of a perpetual dusk.

≈≈≈

Near the junction of Colorado's Dolores and the San Miguel rivers, downstream from granite sided mountains and alkaline basins, there rests a small rainwater pool at the foot of a steep sandstone cliff. To find this pool, the traveler must follow a dry wash, past juniper and piñon, large rectangular boulders of rust and stone, and the occasional prickly pear cactus. On some of the boulders collared lizards blaze turquoise and yellow in the bright sun, and jack-rabbits scatter from the threat of thermal riding red-tailed hawks. As one approaches the north-facing cliff, the air begins to smell of moisture. At last, fighting one's way past a maze of tumbled sandstone slabs, one discovers an amphitheater carved by wind and water in the cliff's side, the high rock walls forming a permanent shadow. Within the amphitheater a small pool rests, a pool that never completely vanishes even in July's blasting heat. Until the time of frost, there are the sounds of insects here – mosquitoes, bumblebees, wasps, and the great black flies that the Navajo believe carry messages from the gods. Occasionally, a canyon wren sings its mysterious, mocking song, a series of clear, descending notes. The mud surrounding the pool holds imprints of mule deer and mountain sheep, and waiting in silence, the traveler will spot mice, pack rats, and an occasional rattlesnake coming down to water.

I have been to this place maybe five or six times. Each time its song deepens.

≈≈≈

In upstate New York, there lies a deep stone channel called Fillmore Glen. Carved by water since the last glaciers receded from the Allegany Plateau, Fillmore Glen is a place of gloomy mysteries. Great hemlock trees loom over the gorge, and here and there massive oaks devour space with their substantial trunks and branches. Running through the gorge, the stream plunges down fifty-foot waterfalls.

One June, after a particularly wet spring, the earth at Fillmore Glen was thoroughly saturated. Water trickled everywhere down the shale walls, and where the cliffs weren't too steep, water drops, clear gems blazing in the sun, illuminated great stretches of hillside ferns.

It was a triumph of water and fecundity.

II

The ancients viewed water as the foundation of the universe. From Pre-Columbian times, the Iroquois pictured the earth resting on a turtle swimming in a vast ocean. The Mayans said that the number "0" represented the ocean, an endless expanse of time and space. They believed that life moved through a succession of five worlds, and that the first world was a world of water. Therefore the first step of their pyramids, the foundational level, represented water. In the first lines of *Genesis*, God enters the void and moves over the waters of the deep before creating light. Or as Lao Tzu, the father of Taoism, proclaimed:

The Way is a void,
Used but never filled:
An abyss it is,
Like an ancestor
From which all things come. . . .
A deep pool it is,
Never to run dry!

In Taoism, water is the most powerful element, wearing down mountains and determining the architecture of the earth. In his essay "The Flow of the River," Loren Eiseley writes, "If there is magic on this planet, it is contained in water. . . . Its substance reaches everywhere; it touches the past and prepares the future; it moves under the poles and wanders thinly in the heights of the air. It can assume forms of exquisite perfection in a snowflake, or strip the living to a single shining bone cast up by the sea."

Water continuously transforms and is in turn transformed. The Zodiacal sign of Aquarius, the water bearer, signals the decay of old forms and the birth of new ones, and bears a relationship to the Tarot card Temperance, its winged angel standing with one foot in the water and one foot on the earth, pouring water from one chalice to another, evoking the Gnostic practice of using two chalices to celebrate the Eucharist – one filled with water and one with wine – which would be ceremoniously poured together.

Inspired by the Gnostics, Carl Jung viewed water as a manifestation of the abyss, a symbol of the deep unconscious that unites us all. Water has long been the realm of dreams and the unconscious. When Odysseus made his ten year voyage across the sea to return to Ithaca and Penelope, he encountered nightmare monsters torn straight from the nether regions of the unconscious, like one-eyed

Polyphemus, the bird-women called the Sirens, the watery vortex of Charybdis, and the multi-headed sailor-devouring Scylla. Even more significant are the goddesses and mortal women who act as Odysseus's seers and protectors, Jung's anima guides to the inner psychic labyrinth – Athena, Circe, Calypso, Leucothea, Nausicaä, Euryclea, and ultimately Penelope herself.

Therefore, from ancient times to the present, the connection between water, the unconscious, mythology, and dreams is clear and powerful.

Whenever I sleep near water, especially outside in a tent or under the stars, my dreams become strange and potent, as if the water pulls up the deep material, the dreams that develop in the roots of the soul, Jung's collective unconscious. I suspect that this is due in part to my not living near water. I imagine that for people who live by the sea, a great lake, or a river, this effect becomes more subtle, and spreads out over thousands of nights and countless dreams. However, I have almost always lived surrounded by the solid earth, and therefore when I do sleep near a major body of water, vivid and profound dreams result. These dreams often signal major life transformations.

IIII

When I was a teen, my Uncle Tony, a powerful man with an outsize torso who could single-handedly wrestle a bull into a truck trailer, would every summer take his nephews camping on the islands of the St. Lawrence River. I loved these trips – the drive north through wooded valleys and hills to the banks of the river, loading the old wood frame motorboat, backing the boat into the water, and then drifting off into the broad stream of the St. Lawrence, carved 30,000 years ago by the bursting of an inland glacial dyke, one of the world's great floods.

On the river, we would enter a wondrous world of cold, clear water smoothly pouring past hundreds of islands, like the Aegean coast compressed into a mile-wide channel. Dense stands of pines and spruce covered most of the islands, though occasionally a private island held grand houses with white porticoes, like apparitions from a Fitzgerald novel. After maybe an hour of cutting our way through the water, we would arrive at an island that was a state park, where we would find a campsite near the sharp, high cliffs. From there, we could see for miles upriver.

On one of these trips, I stayed up past the others. It was a moonless, summer midnight, and up there on the Canadian border the air was already cool. In one tent, my uncle slept alone, and I could just make out the quiet murmuring of his transistor radio, the one he kept on evenings because he could only sleep to its electronic whisperings. In the other tent, which I shared with my cousin Bob, he was already wrapped up in his sleeping bag, quietly snoring. The fire at my feet pulsed with its last embers, a red-orange world slowly dying. Above, stars filled the sky's depths, the Milky Way a glowing arc bisecting the dark heavens, while a quiet wind moved through the heavy spruce branches. As for me, it was the summer between high school and college, and I was thinking about the great changes to come.

Finally, my gaze settled onto the embers, and during the long, smoky minutes I grew tired. So, after dousing the fire, I crawled into my tent, slid into my sleeping bag, and crossed over into the territory of sleep.

Much later, when it was nearly first light, I dreamt of the turquoise planet.

I had been experiencing dreams of this world for several years. In the usual version, I would awaken around three a.m. at my parents' rural home, leave my bedroom, descend the century old stairs, pass through the white pillars of the front porch, and enter the dark hayfields across the dirt road. There, looking to the northeast, I would spy a blue-green orb, about the size of a pea held in one's palm, floating above the grey horizon in the star-mad sky.

That night on the St. Lawrence, the turquoise planet took on monstrous proportions. In my dream, I awoke to discover a blue-green light bathing the tent. Pulling myself out of the sleeping bag in one fluid motion, an impossible act in real life, I passed through the tent opening without unzipping the mosquito netting. Outside, the sky was ablaze with stars, but in unrecognizable constellations, as if I had awoken on a planet circling an alien sun. The light was coming from my left, past a steep hill covered with pines.

Wanting to find the source, I entered the forest and began to climb. The way was difficult, and I kept stumbling on logs hidden in shadow. A few times I spotted pairs of yellow eyes in the tangled evergreens. Ahead, the light poured through the branches, back-lighting them, creating a matrix of thick, ink-black lines and angles. Occasional boulders loomed like hunched bears. At last I reached the summit and broke through to a granite cliff which plunged straight down into the river.

And there before me, igniting the river with its blue-green light, hovered an immense orb, ten times the size of the full moon. Its surface was featureless, a mighty turquoise sphere ascending ponderously past a broken horizon formed by river and islands. When its full circular form was revealed, I felt as if I were falling into it, and threw up my arms in fear.

I woke up for real to a totally dark tent. My arms were out of the sleeping bag, raised straight in the air. As I came to consciousness, my arms dropped across my chest. The air was cold, and the tent smelled musty and damp. I could hear my cousin breathe deeply in his sleep. Outside, a bird made a tentative call to the sky. Dawn was near.

This was the last time I dreamed of the turquoise planet.

Today, regarding this series of dreams through a Jungian lens, I believe they were generated by my transition from adolescence to young adulthood. The turquoise planet stood in for the *lapis exilis* – the philosopher's stone of alchemical metamorphosis representing the extreme life change I was undergoing. The spherical shape of the planet was a symbol for completion, an image of the fully developed adult psyche for which I was striving.

≈≈≈

About fifteen years later, I had another powerful dream brought on by water. At the time I was living in Santa Fe, but the dream did not take place in New Mexico.

One day, following an urge to visit San Francisco, I packed some things, got in my white Toyota pick-up, and started out at high noon for the Pacific coast. The hours rolled past as I drove, coffee fueled, through Albuquerque, Gallup, and Flagstaff. Darkness fell before Kingman, and total darkness enveloped Barstow. After a bleary-eyed five a.m. breakfast in Bakersfield, I pushed on, staying on Route 58 to cross the beige waves of the Temblor Range at sunrise. By the time I reached Santa Margarita on U.S. 101, I knew I could go only a short ways before collapsing. So, I carefully negotiated the streets of San Luis Obispo and made my way to Morro Bay. There, with the blazing mid-morning sun to my back, I faced the sea, dull green army surplus sleeping bag tucked under one arm.

To the south stood Morro Rock, and across from it rose the Morro Bay power plant with its great white rectangular buildings and three white smoke stacks tapering into the sun's blaze. Not wanting the plant in my view of the world before sliding into sleep, I headed north along the beach, searching for a sheltered spot. Beside me, the ocean rolled in, beige and grey towards the shore, slate streaked with turquoise further out. After about fifteen minutes of wandering, I found a hollow formed from sand and beach grasses where I rolled out my sleeping bag and crawled inside. Over the small humps of sand past my feet, I could just make out the breakers coming in, and I watched the waves for a time as the sky grew brighter. Maybe three dozen waves tumbled in before I fell asleep.

This dream started the moment I closed my eyes.

I was back in my house in Santa Fe, an old single-story adobe about four blocks from the plaza. My wife of those days – tall, solid in an athletic way, with long brown hair – was doing the dishes in the kitchen, while I was leaning against the blue-painted wall next to 1950's era gas stove. We talked for a time, and then I walked down the short hallway into the living room, a cubical space with walls made from bumpy stucco and cracked windows repaired with tape. Just past the hallway, there stood a brown steel gas stove about the size of a small freezer topped by a galvanized pipe running up through the roof. As I walked out of the hallway, I noticed something to my right.

I was shocked to see a man of about sixty years of age sitting in the hard-backed chair we kept in the corner next to the stove. Dressed in a white suit with a dark maroon tie, he possessed an almost skeletal face. His close-cropped grey hair left his high forehead exposed to the ceiling light. He wore circular wire-frame glasses, held a polished oak walking stick, and looked up at me with a mocking smile and piercing blue eyes.

"Who are you?" I managed to get out with great effort, fear seizing my throat. "What are you doing here?"

"I am here to tell you to stop compromising," he said in stern, German accented words. "You must write. Stop fooling around. Get to it!"

Upon barking this command, he began to rise, placing his weight on his walking stick. I wanted to retreat into the kitchen, but I was paralyzed. My fear of this mysterious man reached an unbearable pitch as he gained his feet and began to walk towards me. Just then, I woke up.

For perhaps ten minutes the dream remained more vivid than the breakers and beach grasses I could see right before me. I knew that the strange man waiting for me in my living room was the German novelist Hermann Hesse, and the dream sequence itself was an echo from the scene in Hesse's *Steppenwolf* in which the autobiographical main character, Harry Haller, has a dream of the poet Goethe.

Steppenwolf takes place in the tumultuous decade of the 1920's. One evening, Haller is having dinner with an old friend, a professor of mythology. It is an uncomfortable affair. The professor has become in the years since their last meeting a vocal reactionary. He rants on about how the "Jews and the Communists" are ruining Germany and criticizes a writer named Harry Haller – certainly no relation to his guest, he assumes – who has attacked the Kaiser and blamed Germany for World War I. When Haller does not respond, for he is indeed the Harry Haller of whom the professor speaks, the professor tries to discuss their favorite topic from old times – Haller's theory of a connection between Mithras and Krishna. But Haller does not take up the topic. The horrors of the war have driven such concerns from his soul.

At last, Haller, who can no longer bear the poisonous hypocrisy of the evening, insults a bust of Goethe, one of the prized possessions of the professor's wife, for being too sanctimonious. Wounded, she flees the room, and Haller, after revealing that he is indeed the Harry Haller who attacked the Kaiser in print, takes leave of the shocked professor and plunges into the dark night.

After this disastrous evening, Haller decides to go through with an earlier decision to commit suicide with a straight razor. He begins to head for his apartment, but his fear of death shakes his resolve. Struggling with his dread of the razor, he wanders the maze of streets in the city's medieval district, occasionally entering a tavern and having a brandy before plunging back into the urban labyrinth.

At last he enters a tavern unknown to him called the Black Eagle. Filled with crowds, smoke, and wild jazz – it's the kind of place he normally avoids. Yet, undeterred, he makes his way to a table where he joins a slender, dark-haired woman. She is Hermine, his feminine doppelganger and forthcoming guide to the bohemian underground. She orders them glasses of burgundy, and as the wine settles the aging writer, Hermine teases out the story of the failed supper with the professor, Haller's disdain for the bust of Goethe, and his desire to kill himself. When she goes off to dance, she tells him to take a nap, and he obeys her deep, maternal voice, and slips into a profound sleep. This is when Haller dreams of Goethe.

In the dream, Haller is a reporter sitting in an 18th century era antechamber waiting to interview Goethe. Feeling a growing nervousness at seeing the great man, he spots a scorpion crawling up his leg. Haller shakes the creature off, but is uncertain where it is hiding. He becomes increasingly paranoid about the scorpion, and begins to associate it with sin and the feminine. As time passes, the scorpion grows larger in Haller's imagination, and he connects it with Molly, the beloved lover praised in the poems by Gottfried August Büger, a German romanticist.

Finally, a servant leads Haller into Goethe's presence. Exuding an aura of authority, the author of *Faust* is nevertheless a short man. A gold star of some honorary order decorates his chest. Goethe accuses Haller's generation of not appreciating the romantics, and Haller responds that they cannot because the romantics embraced the illusion that life and spiritual striving have meaning. The two discuss Mozart's *The Magic Flute*, and Goethe observes that whether one dies in one's eighties, as Goethe did, or in one's thirties, as did Mozart, death is death, and the time comes when "there must be enough of play."

A series of metamorphoses then unfold – Goethe changes into a young man who looks like Mozart, the honorary star turns into a bouquet of wildflowers, a miniature effigy of a woman's leg becomes the scorpion, and finally Goethe becomes a thousand years old, laughing throughout his transformation. Haller awakens at his table, surprised that he could have slept in the noisy tavern.

It was all there – falling asleep in unusual surroundings, the dream encounter with an admired author, the feelings of fear and consternation brought on by the author's presence, and the command to write, to devote one's life to the sacred work of producing art. Thus, my dream Hesse's order to "Get to it!" had its source in Goethe's pronouncement that, "Sooner or later there must be enough of play."

And on either side of these dreams stands the goddess. For Haller this is Hermine, a young, vital figure, sensuous and filled with life, who guides Haller out of his maze of depression and leads him on strange paths through the postwar world of drugs, jazz, and cabarets. And for me it was the sea, where Odysseus encountered Circe, Calypso, and Nausicaä; and Theseus met the sea-goddess Amphitrite, who in one version of the Minotaur legend, gives him the glowing wreath that guides him through the Minoan labyrinth. Therefore, the sea had acted as my guide, bringing me a dream Hesse who ordered me to write, a craft I had been neglecting.

For a while I closed my eyes, feeling the warm sun on my body, hearing the steady rhythm of the waves, smelling the seaweed and baked sand. I thought I might fall asleep again, but my mind and heart were restless, so I rolled up my sleeping bag and got into my pick-up. Starting the engine, I wound my way out of the parking lot and turned north on California Route 1, heading for San Francisco.

≈≈≈

Nearly twenty years later, I was driving up that same stretch of highway, passing through the heart of Big Sur. This time I was traveling with my daughters – Ursula, aged 13, and Isadora, two years younger. We'd spent the day swimming at the very same beach where Hermann Hesse had visited me in a dream and commanded me to write, an order I have followed ever since. California's coastal waters are too cold for my taste, so I had lounged in the sun while the girls, rather skinny in their bright one-piece bathing suits, their long blond hair tied back in pony-tails, gathered mounds of seaweed and odd pieces of driftwood that looked like totems from a forgotten civilization.

As we drove along the winding highway, edging the sea cliffs and shooting out across canyons on narrow bridges held aloft by slender concrete arches, the clouds rolled in and became steadily heavier, lower, darker. For the first thirty miles we pulled off at overlooks, eager for views of the vast, slate-colored sea, but when the rains came, spraying the windshield and darkening the shale and granitic rocks, we just stayed in the car and kept heading north. We were in my decade-old Honda Civic, which had a tendency to steam up inside. The defrost was running full blast, the windows were cracked open, and I still had to wipe the inside of the windshield with an increasingly wet rag.

Under these conditions, the driving wore me down, and by the time we reached the town of Big Sur, dusk was nearly finished, and I was too. We found a place that rented cabins and took one for the night. The girls, exhausted from their day of swimming, were soon asleep, but I sat on the pine cabin's front porch until nearly midnight. The rain had slowed to a steady drizzle, and the surrounding redwoods were dripping with water. Scattered mercury vapor lamps lit up the forest, and I could see the trees quite well up to the canopy. It was a wondrous, green world, filled with dripping spruce branches, stained red-brown trunks, and the scattered cabins, each with its yellow porch light glowing mysteriously in the pine darkness. This place was a sharp contrast to the desert where I dwell, and I was captivated by the night mists, the dark green life, the musty smell of a forest floor saturated with water.

I had a lot on my mind that night. I was at the end of a four year relationship, one that had been deeply close and emotional. But it was breaking up, and worried about the future, I struggled with accepting the disintegration. Therefore, it was natural that a powerful dream awaited me, and the day's images of water – the sea, the rain, the dripping forest – were the alchemical catalyst that unleashed my unconscious.

The dream emerged soon after I turned off the small bedside lamp and slid into the covers. Strangely, however, my dream was about the dry plains of Africa.

At this time, my father had been gone for over a quarter of a century. When he died at fifty-nine, he already had a full head of white hair and a thick grey mustache. However, in my dream, he was a vigorous thirty, with curly black hair cropped short and a clipped mustache.

Looking and acting like a Slavic Douglas Fairbanks, he was driving a jeep, barreling down a dirt road that crossed the African veldt. My daughters and I were his passengers. The sun was blazing, and a harsh white light illuminated a landscape of scattered, dusty green trees and spiky plants. Behind us, the jeep kicked up great dust plumes as we sped along a row of mysterious adobe mounds. Now and then, my father would turn at a mound, and beyond would stand a village of conical mud huts with thatched roofs where we would screech to a stop.

From the huts, people would emerge – solemn men with spears, women carrying babies, laughing children, wise crones, and male elders with long staffs of office, who conferred with my father in low, authoritative tones. Then, with great dignity, my father would shake each elder's hand and then run back to the jeep, leap in, and take off in a vortex of dust.

"We must help these people," he would shout above the roar of the engine, grinning like Zorro facing great odds. Somehow, I knew my father was in charge of protecting the land from drought, disease, swarms of locusts, and other de-structive acts of nature. I was impressed by his compassion and power, but most of all by his lively masculine energy – so different from my more introverted, intellectual persona.

After visiting a half-dozen villages, we shot over a vast rift valley on a mas-sive stone bridge that looked like a Roman aqueduct. To my alarm, the structure began collapsing behind us, its great cut blocks tumbling down and smashing to pieces on the valley floor. My father just laughed. "Now we can't go back!" he shouted over the jeep engine and the sounds of shattering rock and masonry.

Waking abruptly, I was confused by the sounds of dripping water and by the dark room lit only by a vague glow coming in through the curtained window, so it took me a moment to remember I was in Big Sur, not in an African veldt or back home in my western Colorado desert. But I was not confused by the dream. Transmitted through my father, a symbol of life's vitality, its meaning was clear: though I might be tempted to try, I must not turn back and attempt to rebuild the life that was crumbling behind me. I must push forward into my new, un-known life, whatever that would be.

IV

A year later, on a bright October day, I came to Colorado's Dominquez Canyon with Brenda – a woman of compassion, beauty, and great intellect – who is today my wife. In that place, there are two converging sandstone valleys, and in places, the Dominquez creek carves past the rust-red sandstone into dark basaltic granite infused with crystal, some of the oldest rock in the world. At one point in the northern canyon, the creek runs across this granite, shaping smooth stone channels through which water pours over a high cliff, forming a waterfall, alive and shining in the high desert sun. It was there, on that autumn day, as we watched the water plunge into the great pool below, that we knew our separate lives were flowing into one. And thus, the new world foretold by my father in the Big Sur dream had become real.

As the sun moved towards the western horizon, changing from white to yellow to deep orange, we knew we had to return to the city where we lived. Reluctantly, we stood and crossed over stream channels carved in granite formed almost at the planetary dawn – the deepest strata of earthly time, the realm of dreams, the collective unconscious. Brenda – slender, lithe, with fine blond features – took the lead as we climbed up the eroded granite slopes back to the trail, which we followed past red cliff walls and golden cottonwoods. Here and there, the trail crossed veins of quartz, their surfaces broken into thousands of fragments that glittered like scattered gems.

At last, we reached the conjunction of the Dominquez Creek and the Gunnison River, known to the Ute Indians as the Tomichi, which originates over a hundred miles east in the Sawatch Mountains and descends from those 13,000 foot heights to carve the Black Canyon, one of the deepest chasms of North America. After traversing the Black Canyon, the Gunnison crosses the wide Uncompahgre Valley and then shapes a passage through the northeastern reaches of the Uncompahgre Plateau, forming a sinuous canyon longer than the Black, but not as deep.

This was where we now stood, together, watching the reflection of light and color on the river's surface, witnessing the power of water – both as a physical element and as a manifestation of the unconscious – to shape landscapes, give birth to dreams, and propel our very lives towards an unknown destination.

John Nizalowski
Biography

Born and raised in upstate New York, John Nizalowski moved to Santa Fe in the mid-1980's and has ever after lived west of the 100th meridian. He is the author of five books: the multi-genre work entitled *Hooking the Sun*; two collections of poetry, *The Last Matinée* and *East of Kayenta*; and two volumes of essays, *Land of Cinnamon Sun* and *Chronicles of the Forbidden*. Nizalowski has also published widely in a variety of literary journals, most notably *Under the Sun, Weber Studies, Puerto del Sol, Slab, Measure, Digital Americana,* and *Blue Mesa Review.* Currently, he teaches mythology, creative writing, and composition at Colorado Mesa University. His blog, Dispatches from the Land of Cinnamon Sun, can be found at http://johnnizalowski.blogspot.com/